D1810519

Murdered Heiress . . . Living Witness

Dr. Petti Wagner

New Wine Press

Copyright © 1988 New Wine Press

Originally published in English under the title
MURDERED HEIRESS ... LIVING WITNESS
Faith and Works, Inc.
By Dr. Olive Peet (Petti) Wagner
P.O.Box 772075
Houston, Texas 77215 - 2075
1984. All rights reserved.

ISBN 0 947852 42 5

All Scripture quotations are taken from the King James Bible Version unless otherwise indicated as follows:

NEB - The New English Bible (Oxford University Press, Copyright © 1961, 1970).

NIV - The New International Version of the Holy Bible (Zondervan Bible Publishers, Copyright © 1973, 1978). British usage Edition published by Hodder & Stoughton.

TLB - The Living Bible (Tyndale House Publishers, Copyright © 1971).

All rights reserved. No part of this book may be reproduced without permission from the publisher, except by a reviewer who may quote brief passages in a review; nor may any part of this book be reproduced, stored in a retrieval system or copied by mechanical, photocopying, recording or other means, without permission from the publisher.

Although the accounts presented herein are factual, some names and details have been changed purposely to disguise scenes and/or protect innocent people. Some items were altered to avoid hurting family members of those involved parties who are now deceased.

There is no such place as Southwest General Hospital in Houston, for example. Those in the Galveston Bay area of Texas will have no trouble recognizing the actual hospital, but to publish the name would harm the reputation of one of the owners who now is involved in a well-known Christian organization.

Dr. Ronald Holmes is a fictitious epithet, though - once again - Houstonians will recognize him. Because of legal provisions, however, the liabilities of naming him outweigh the benefits.

Zelda, David, George, Don, Dr. Barnes - all are real people, but have aliases. Their families already have suffered enough.

Dedication:

to Peter and Kimberli — with love

Dr. Petti Wagner has been a regular, faithful member of the body of believers at Lakewood Church for many years. She is highly respected and loved. I do not think any single person in the congregation brings more people to the services and introduces them to Jesus than Dr. Wagner! The person might be someone she meets on the street — a congressman, a judge, a doctor, a lawyer, or some business executive. They all need Jesus, and she does her best to help them understand His love and compassion.

Be prepared to face the supernatural as you read Dr. Wagner's almost unbelievable true story. She did indeed endure a horrible death experience, but through God's mercy, she has been given back her life to serve Jesus and help suffering humanity.

The account of the intervention of God's supernatural power in behalf of this extraordinary woman will strengthen your faith and help you realize that God is interested in each of us.

Remember the words of Jesus: "With men this is impossible; but with God all things are possible" (Matthew 19:26).

John Osteen
Pastor
Lakewood Church
Houston, Texas

Acknowledgments:

to Gerald and Tinky Mackey — my dear friends and spiritual parents, for their constant love and patient support in their willingness to stop everything at hand, despite the hour, and to tackle any problems or questions from this new, inquisitive, child of God.

to Martha Brady Bruton and Betty Buchanan — who were sent at just the right time when I most needed them for moral support and encouragement. Their consistent urging and prodding spurred this book into existence.

to Jerry Hamilton — whose every step in my behalf was ordered by the Lord. If God had blessed me with another son, he would have been just like Jerry.

Murdered Heiress...
Living Witness

Contents

Page

Foreword. 1
1 Crayon Trap 5
2 Silver Spoon. 11
3 Lady With The Golden Touch 16
4 Tarnish 21
5 All That Glitters 32
6 Shadowy Valley. 41
7 Death Chamber. 56
8 Red Ribbons. 62
9 Return to Prison 68
10 The Spoon. 75
11 Freedom 80
12 Land Of The Living. 91
13 Tangled Web. 113
14 Devastation 128
15 Wine Of Hatred, Taste Of Greed 133
16 Shekinah. 147
17 Restoration 155
18 Threads In The Tapestry. 158
19 Crash Course 168
20 My Son, My Son 176
21 A New Woman. 179
22 Preparations 187
23 Vengeance. 190
24 Living Witness. 199

Foreword

The human spirit, with some unique individuals, has a power to survive, overcome and be victorious. It is greater than the cruelty of fear and pain and even the authority of death.

This is the story of such an extraordinary person — a victim of a nightmarish horror. It is a truthful account of her abduction, torture and death.

How did she survive? How was she able to escape? How was she able to overcome and be victorious?

Is it worth your time to read it?

I think so.

This book is an incredible story about Dr. Petti Wagner, a fantastic person. I was her observer — a participant and a beneficiary — and was inspired by her struggle. To be her comrade in arms was to be warmed by a fire, to see more clearly because the light was stronger.

What are the chances for the survival of one little woman — unaccustomed to rude behavior — when clever thieves conspire to abduct, rob and eliminate her? The odds are about 100 to 1 in favor of the adversaries. Those who are willing to destroy for their own gain always find allies among the professions, people who are happy to oppress the innocent and champion the cause of the guilty — for adequate payment.

In order to win this contest, Petti Wagner had to survive to escape, had to escape to save her life and had to fight her way through the courts to overcome and be victorious. Each step she took is unbelievable but in this story you start with the unbelievable and go on from there.

She was to be like a new car set upon by thieves — stolen, stripped and burned. Their plan was so clever and simple. How could it fail?

Who has the least credibility of anyone in our society? A patient in a psychiatric hospital! Where in our society is a person most likely to die and arouse the least suspicion? A hospital! That was their method. What they did to her was unbelievable.

An innocent victim, she had only one method for her struggle — to fight back, overcome and be victorious. It was a poor method. In dealing with the cunning and unprincipled adversary she had to comply with a rigid system of strict principles to obtain the proof she needed. While she had the principles, her adversaries had the evidence and were free to destroy or deny it.

This procedure was expensive, lengthy and emotionally consuming. This method is the justice system of our civil courts. I know about it. I am a lawyer.

I had just started practicing law when I met Petti Wagner. I believed her when she told me how she escaped from the psychiatric hospital. I had my reservations for quite a while about her returning from the dead; now I have no question about it. We took on, as our adversaries, these officials and institutions which were the instruments of her pain and death. The principals who would have seen her dead paid for their actions. Some paid with their lives and for some the payment was simply their money and reputations.

How did Petti Wagner — small in stature and with no physical strength, money, powerful friends or allies — escape from double-padlocked isolation, resist and overcome brain-searing electrocution and convince a skeptical society with truth and conviction? She has a *mighty* soul!

The purpose of this book is not to relate the violent murder conspiracy. It reminds us that what is right will always survive in some fashion in a contest with evil. It confirms our belief that there is a purpose and a reason for everything. Most important, it shows that a nightmare may become a dream — that from cruel adversity may come courage, peace and joy.

**Jerry J. Hamilton
Attorney at Law
Houston, Texas**

CHAPTER 1

Crayon Trap

"Dr. Wagner!" the husky voice on the telephone urgently began, "your Aunt Anna has just suffered a heart attack!"

I had been preparing to leave my Dorrington Drive penthouse/office complex when the jangling phone interrupted me with the shattering news about my precious 81-year-old aunt. I noticed the clock — 8 p.m. It was Monday, March 8, 1971.

"She has been taken to the Southwest Hospital on Westheimer Road," the voice continued. "Can you come immediately? She needs you desperately! She will be in Room 120."

Click! The incessant tone only added to my tumultuous thoughts.

I was dressed for an elegant dinner with Lana, a dear friend and former employee. I had looked forward to spending a few hours over Houston's best cuisine, rekindling our friendship and getting away from some of the pressures of my business.

My recently-purchased black slinky pantsuit was accented by some of my most expensive jewelry, and though I had hardly ever considered myself a stunning beauty, with my raven hair and slender 110-pound figure, I knew I could still turn a few male heads.

Yet, I had to react immediately. No choice! As I rushed out to my car, I called over my shoulder to my friend, "Wait for me! Don't leave until I get back."

There's always so much to do," I thought as I jumped behind the steering wheel of my white Cadillac. "I can't forget to drop today's receipts at the bank when I come back to pick up Lana," I made a hurried mental note, remembering approximately $3000 of checks and cash I carried in my purse.

"Room 120 ... Southwest Hospital ... Westheimer Road ..." my mind raced. I knew the way. It was right next to my Aunt Anna's doctor's office, and I had often taken her to his office for checkups.

Then the enormity of the telephone call began to explode. No longer was I thinking of my plans or pantsuit or friend. I knew I had to get to my aunt. She was the only living relative in Houston from my former husband's family. She had been my counselor, my mother (since my own died some years before), my friend. She was a little Baptist woman, plucky and precious. I wanted her to live!

"But why Southwest?" I asked out loud as I raced out of the parking lot. "Why would her doctor admit her in that horrible place?" Even though it was convenient to her physician's office, it still seemed the worst choice for emergency care. So many reports of questionable patient treatment and staff incompetency there had seethed for months through Houston. As the shady reputation had grown, the hospital seemed increasingly empty. And though lenient Texas health care policies allowed the hospital to remain open, there were many rumors circulating of impending bankruptcy.

"Hardly the place for my aunt!" I fumed. I knew what I had to do. As soon as I arrived, I would immediately arrange for her transfer over to St. Luke's. There I knew, absolutely, that she would receive the best possible care. And if, as the telephone call insisted, she had suffered a heart attack, I knew at St. Luke's that she would receive the best cardiac care from my long-time friend, a world-famous heart specialist.

Driving through Houston, I pushed the accelerator to dangerous speeds, hoping that my white convertible would attract a policeman who could then escort me to the hospital. I saw none, so I went as quickly as possible by myself.

Even as I hastily parked outside the hospital, I couldn't help noticing that the lot was almost completely deserted. That confirmed many of my fears; I knew I *must* get Aunt Anna away from that place, at all costs.

Rushing into the lobby, I was immediately aware of an eerie stillness. The front lobby desk was unattended, and no one was in sight, not even a nurse.

Directly in front of my eyes, I saw a makeshift sign hanging on the wall. Printed on it with a bright red crayon-marker was "Room 120" and an arrow pointing down a long hallway to my right.

"Hmmm," I wondered. There were some building materials in the hallways, so I figured that the intensive care unit must have moved, and that the lettered sign indicated where the emergency patients were. Still, it seemed very strange.

I hurried down the hall to the end of the building, briefly noticing that all the rooms seemed empty. It was getting more spooky by the moment.

"I've got to get her out of this place!"

At the end of the hallway, I found another marker, similar to the first one, and an arrow pointing up a stairway to the second floor. Another sign on the second level directed me up still another flight of stairs.

"Room 120 — on the third floor?" I was torn between bolting back down the stairs and out of the building and going forward as directed to the intensive care ward (wherever it had been moved). I was mostly worried and exasperated, filled with disgust at such ineptness and unconcern.

"Poor Aunt Anna." She had been like a grandmother to Peter and Kimberli, my children. I left them with her often when I traveled. Whenever I bought anything for myself — a new washing machine, a fur coat, or a new kitchen gadget — I almost always bought two, one for her. We had been so close.

"And now she's in this!" It seemed unthinkable.

Hurrying out into the third-floor corridor, I saw more lumber and remodeling debris scattered about the floor.

Then, far down the hall I saw two men, one tall and extremely overweight and one more normal-sized. Both were dressed in hospital whites and standing next to the entrance of a room.

"Great!" I silently exclaimed. "They are probably ambulance attendants!" How lucky I felt to have arrived before they left. I would get Aunt Anna transferred to St. Luke's without any delay, and they could take care of it immediately.

Over the doorway where they stood was another sign, the then-familiar "Room 120" proclaimed in bold red.

"At least I've found her. Now ..."

Rushing past the attendants, I entered the room. The bed was empty. I was confused and out of breath from so much stair-climbing. I was also quickly losing my patience with the run-down conditions of the place.

I whirled around. Then I saw that the two white-uniformed men had followed me inside.

"I must be in the wrong room!" I spoke quickly. "I'm looking for Anna Carnes, my aunt."

"And who are you?" boomed the largest of the two, his steel-dark eyes and thunder-filled voice sending an unexpected wave of terror shuddering through me. Steel-and-Thunder stood at least six and a half feet tall, and his blubbery body had to weigh well over 300-pounds. All the years with my nutrition and weight-loss clinic helped me size up people that way quickly. This time, I didn't like what I saw at all.

I shifted away from his strange gaze and looked searchingly into his sidekick's face. The shorter of the two, he still towered over my small five-two frame.

I knew there was surely some logical explanation for Aunt Anna's absence from the room, that there was no reason for my bothersome fears, and that the men were probably there to help me.

Quickly, I responded to the question — "I am Dr. Petti Wagner, Anna Carnes' niece."

Both men grinned strangely. Steel-and-Thunder's eyes narrowed as he hissed, "Well, you're in the right room, Dr. Wagner..."

Before I could speak again, my head exploded as his massive fist smacked my left temple. Another strike slung me onto the hard floor and I crumpled on the far side of the bed.

Everything began unfolding like a sickening, slow-motion sequence. With my ears ringing and my consciousness already blurring, I lifted my head just as Sidekick's boot swung, knocking me against the wooden floor once more.

The room swirled around me. A piercing pain throbbed through my brain. I had suddenly been submerged in horrible terror and bewilderment. I kept thinking, "There has to be some mistake!"

The stomping continued. I tried to shield my head

with my arms and cried for them to stop, but the pounding came wave after wave.

I tried to scream, but my ears rang with such excruciating pain that I couldn't tell whether any sound came from my mouth. I was pressed against the floor.

I felt myself strangling, spitting out salty fluid mixed with sharp bits of broken teeth. Streaming blood poured from my left eye. Nausea swept over me. I knew I was going to die. Whatever the reason, I just wanted it to be over. The pain was too intense.

Then, as abruptly as it had begun, the barrage ceased. Each man grabbed one of my arms. Together, they yanked me to a sitting position beside the bed.

A white-uniformed woman stood close-by. She just added to the unbelievable hell in which I found myself. An absurd, comic-strip nurse caricature — old, skinny, thinning hair gathered into a little wad on top of her head — she produced a hypodermic syringe, grabbed my right arm, jabbed the needle right through my black jersey blouse, and squeezed the contents into me.

I fought to get free, to escape; but resistance was worse than useless. Vice-like grips on my arms held me tightly. My continued screams were only echoed inside the four walls.

Almost immediately, a strange numbness coursed through my body, spreading from my neck and through my limbs.

On signal, the three released me and started toward the door, but I crawled after them screaming —"There has to be some mistake!"

I beat on the door until my knuckles bled, then pounded with the heel of my boot; but it did no good. Soul-shattering pain and the sound of voices outside the door let me know I was still alive.

I heard the dead bolt click into place. The room swam around me. Then I lost consciousness, isolated in my own private hell.

CHAPTER 2

Silver Spoon

Nothing in my 56 years before that fateful March 1971 evening had prepared me for the trauma which was just beginning.

I was born with the proverbial silver spoon in my mouth. Given the rather cumbersome name, Daisy Olive Peet, I was the fourth child of twelve born to descendants of the well-known Peet family.

As one of the heirs of the Peet fortune, as namesake of my paternal grandmother (Olive), and as the object of my paternal grandfather's special favor, I wanted for nothing. There was no need for childish visions of sugarplums; I had dreams at my fingertips. Other children my age wore ugly, black cotton stockings and bloomers, but my sisters and I wore silk.

My family lived in elegant sufficiency with no worries or anxieties. We had very productive land, limousines, spacious homes, and equally affluent relatives. Almost every evening, my family gathered around the huge dining room table, each of us sitting in gracefully carved, cherry chairs. Time practically stood still as we listened to and talked with our handsome, intelligent father and our refined mother. Around that table we were schooled in the social graces, learned to converse intelligently about world affairs, and listened to our parents read the great literature. In many ways, the phrase from Robert Browning's "Pippa Passes," "God's in His Heaven — All's right with the world!" seemed written for our family circle. Those evening sessions only accented the immeasurable wealth and security I felt in our Iowa estate.

I was named for my famous grandmother (which led to the butt end of many hackneyed jokes — "May I hold your Palmolive?" "Not on your Lifebuoy!"), but I had lots of other nicknames. One of my favorites was Petti (pronounced Petey); Daddy told me that Petti meant little and built for speed. That suited me very well, and the name stuck.

All of Mother and Father's nine girls and three boys were unusually precocious, enjoying an extraordinary everyday life.

The only problem, at least for me, was a comparison with my other beautiful sisters. I was the ugly duckling of the family, not stunning in figure and feature like the others. The duckling-syndrome wasn't an emotional scar; rather, it was more of a skin-deep technicality. Thankfully, I had understanding (if a bit too honest) parents. On more than one occasion as we sat around the dining room table, I asked, "Daddy, how could you and God make my eight sisters so beautiful and make me so ugly?" His reply was always the same — "Darlin', we made you beautiful on the *inside.*"

Even ugly ducklings eventually become swans, but I especially believed my father's comments about being beautiful on the inside.

My mother was truly remarkable. With twelve children to manage, she was totally dedicated to instilling the finest qualities into us. She never acknowledged problems, only solutions. The happiest moments came when she gathered us around her while she rocked the youngest, holding us spellbound with one song after the other — "Pretty Red Wing," "Danny Boy," "Wee Bonnie Clyde," "Rock of Ages." Her angelic voice belied an indomitable strength.

Like all children, I fantasized what I would be when I grew up, dreaming about a distinguished career as a diplomat, maybe an ambassador to the Court of St. James, perhaps a female Albert Schweitzer or William Jennings Bryan.

The only conceivable obstacle to the realization of those dreams, it seemed, would be the appearance of a handsome prince who would sweep me off my feet and take me to a lofty castle perched high in the Alps. There, with an army of servants to command, my prince and I would live happily ever after, surrounded by our beautiful children.

Such were the dreams and desires of my idyllic childhood.

At four, I started attending the nearby one-room country school. At five, I made a well-thought-out decision to accept Jesus Christ into my heart. From the time I was quite small, our family regularly attended the neighborhood Congregational Sunday school and church. It was all part of my wonderful, wonderful childhood.

However, soon I began leaving childish things behind. I was ambitious, like all my family, and that burning drive grew. I hated being second best at anything I tackled. I was only fourteen when I finished high school, and, though I was the youngest member of my small high school graduating class, I was honored as the valedictorian.

I was still fourteen when I entered the University.

That, in itself, was a challenge. My Daddy had told each of his children, "You each have to work and pay for your first college degree. After that, I'll pay for any more education you want — anywhere."

Although the silver spoon was temporarily removed, I found an ever-increasing desire to win. My mother and daddy had taught each of us well. It wasn't easy pulling weeds for five cents an hour or working at other jobs for the needed money, but I managed to pay for that first degree. I graduated with honors at eighteen years of age.

During the coming years, I would continue my education, receiving a Master's Degree in Psychology a Ph.D. in Psychology, and a Ph.D. in Medical Research. There would be more later.

Yet, Daddy didn't have to pay for any of that education. By the time I was sixteen, I was already starting to carve out my own destiny.

The reason — I wanted my own life without the silver spoon. *Fortune* Magazine would later quote me as saying, "I'm constantly spurred on by the knowledge that there's no limit to what I can accomplish, if I want it badly enough."

I wanted to succeed, badly. I was no stranger to hard work. I learned from my family what was really important — ninety-nine percent work and only one percent ability. That, not talent or personality, was a major ingredient of success. Another key element was more involved — that every person who had ever been truly successful had centered on forming the habit of doing things others just didn't like to do.

Proud? Perhaps. Maybe even to a fault. I just knew that I *would not* be second best. I had to be more than just an heiress.

Little did I know how far my dreams would take me,

nor how lofty my spiraling success would reach.

CHAPTER 3

Lady With The Golden Touch

Needless to say, when I went to the University it was a tremendous time of change. I was only fourteen, a gangly, dark-haired teenager quite aware that most of my classmates were at least four years older than I.

Socially, I wanted to be accepted, and I was somewhat elated at the attention I received; however, I was also painfully aware of the differences.

Since I really wasn't old enough to join in with much of the typical collegiate pursuits (namely dating), I began doing additional research the first few years at the university. That led to a rather unusual chapter of my life.

Instead of depending upon my family's fortune and their inexhaustible resources, at the age of sixteen I determined to become a success on my own.

Without my parents knowing anything about my endeavor (at first), I applied for and received a small loan ($600), bought the campus beauty salon at the University, and began putting together a profitable venture — for myself, and for the hair stylists I hired. Between my sophomore and junior years, I decided to attend a local beauty school. I didn't necessarily want to get a beautician's license to dress hair for the rest of my life, but I knew that I would be a better businessperson if I knew more about the subject.

It was the ideal business for a young woman, but I had bigger dreams.

With the help of my chemistry professor, I began conducting a series of experiments in the science of hair treatment. Up to that point, curling hair was a monstrous task of metal rollers and ugly, sometimes painful paraphernalia. I felt there had to be a better way. The result was the development of the first cold-wave permanent in the United States.

It was a successful operation, drawing attention from many directions. With the help of a friend, I began marketing the product on a larger scale.

Then, at nineteen, a year after obtaining my master's degree in psychology, I got an exciting, mind-boggling offer from a European firm for rights to the cold-wave venture. When I sold those rights, I suddenly became a teenage millionairess — on my own.

Perhaps it was that Peet pride, but the greatest part of my heady success meant that I would never need the silver spoon again. I fully intended to enjoy my newfound riches. I knew I never would have to work again.

For the next few years, I alternated between traveling the world and going to school (including stints in Zurich, Switzerland, and around the United States).

Again, I never planned to pursue business interests, but when I met the inventor of a wonderful mechanical massage unit, I knew I had stumbled onto something that could help victims of polio *and* make big money at the same time. Like the cold-wave venture (and others yet to come), I always seemed to be able to combine making money and helping people. With the massage unit, the temptation was irresistible. Within five years, Niamco (my company), had an enormous annual sales volume and a huge nationwide sales organization.

I've heard that success breeds success. *Fortune Magazine* later did a feature. Their article was titled, "The Lady with the Golden Touch." I guessed it looked that way. I was well dressed, from an extremely wealthy family, had been somewhat of a scholastic and professional prodigy, and continued to have success in my business ventures.

When I sold my interest in the massage-chair units, I turned my attention to still another field — hydroponics (growing plants without soil). I acquired and began developing a machine that would grow more green feed from any type grain in an eight foot space *every day* than an 83-acre farm could produce in an entire year! With the end of World War II, the government got into the act — the Marshall Plan helped finance the production of equipment to relieve critical food shortages in Europe. My Herbagere machine was tested and approved by leading government livestock officials, agronomists, biologists, and herbalists. Stock raisers, dairymen, and poultry farm operators began installing the machine, reporting results with enthusiastic endorsements. My Niamco (Herbagere) Company profits skyrocketed, and eventually a major corporate network made a staggering offer. When I sold that enterprise, I was again temporarily at loose ends — never for long.

When people kept telling me how smart I was, I knew in my heart that my success was due to many things. First, I had an overwhelming desire to win. Also, I knew that an amazing series of "coincidences" kept putting the right people with me at the right times. I *knew* it was more than pure luck. I gave God the credit, even though I didn't know Him personally.

Mostly, I stayed in hot pursuit of first place, rushing into business after business, carving out an empire for myself. Different merchandising experts sought my advice and counsel. I began market-testing products for companies, developing sales plans, suggesting improvements. It got so I knew almost instinctively whether a product would be successful or if there was something wrong with the system.

I was a world traveler, market analyst, manufacturer, sales consultant, sales manager, and already held several degrees from prestigious universities.

I burned with ambition. More than just being wealthy, I truly wanted to help people — each of my businesses and academic pursuits reflected that desire. In fact, I had made money, lots of it, to overcome the obstacle of my family's wealth — to become a success in my own right. That, to me, was the most satisfying area of anything I had accomplished. That's the real reason why I worked so hard, was so driven. I just didn't realize it at the time.

A national magazine reporter boasted, "Everything that Petti touches turns to gold!" That same article labeled me, "Youthful and dynamic . . . the type of person whose magnetic personality attracts and holds friends, stimulates interest and commands respect."

I did appear to be "The Lady with the Golden Touch." But sometimes looks can be deceiving.

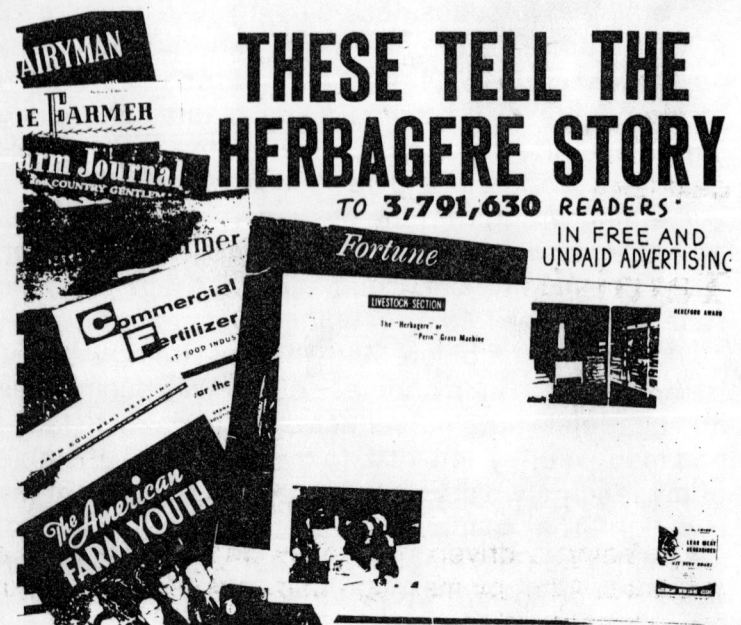

Some of the national media coverage of Petti's Herbagere Company, a corporation she merged with an Incubator Corporation on the American Stock Exchange.

CHAPTER 4

Tarnish

For being a driven businesswoman, I was also a romantic. A happy marriage had always been one of my fondest dreams.

Early in my career, I gave a professor who taught me law and psychology, financial backing which he needed to complete a study on the components of compatibility required for stable marriages. In turn, I used his information as the basis for my doctoral dissertation (psychology).

This study was much ahead of its time, but the material the doctor and I developed produced some significant findings. Scientific matchmaking, psychological testing, and organization of electronic data (though computers were still in embryonic stages) began to make a dent in the growing divorce rates.

Thoroughly equipped to choose a perfect mate for other people (as a Doctor of Psychology), I naturally assumed that I would marry the right man when the time came. I would, as in my childhood dreams, have the ideal "Cinderella" marriage.

I met my "Prince Charming" during the summer of 1945. I was having a fling in the New York City theatrical world. No longer an "ugly duckling," I had convinced myself that I was beautiful. There was no need to convince anyone that I was rich.

Karl Wagner was tall, dark, imperially handsome, and considered quite a catch. He was in business for himself, and had also been trained to be a diplomat. He telephoned me from time to time until I agreed to go out with him. We were quite compatible on an intellectual level. He was suave, debonair, traveled, a good dancer, and a complete gentleman. In the dizzying whirl of courtship which ensued, I thought that we were right for each other. In 1946, we were married in a quiet ceremony, moved to Dayton, Ohio, and set out to live happily ever after.

I continued to work hard and study, still determined to be a success in marriage and business. Karl became president of all my business enterprises, and we moved to Little Rock.

In 1948, a challenging opportunity arose for us to move to Houston, Texas. Some Houston officials learned of the work I had financed for the college professor and of my dissertation on the subject of marital compatibility. At that time, Houston had the highest divorce rate of any city in the nation. Alarmed, city officials sought ways to thwart the growing, tragic statistics. They felt that my pervious work qualified me as a marriage-compatibility expert and invited me to that booming city to help reverse the trend. The result was the establishment of Maritronics International, the only legitimate dating service in the city.

Since it was impossible to magically cure shaky marriages, I focused my attention on helping singles find the right mates. It was simply a matter of spotlighting a solution instead of merely stroking the symptoms.

"Simply" probably isn't the correct word to use in context with Maritronics. It quickly became a complex operation. Persons interested in finding suitable dates — and marriage partners — came in droves. With information supplied from a battery of psychological tests and in-depth interviews with clients, they were then matched, based on the compatibility components I had developed.

The number of happy marriages caused the service provided by Maritronics to be successful beyond my wildest dreams. I began hiring other psychiatrists, physicians, and counselors to help me. Divorce statistics in the city of Houston began a marked decline. The thousands of harmonious marriages drew national attention.

Everyone was happy, it seemed, except me. My golden touch was starting to tarnish. My ability to solve marital problems for others didn't help me with my own.

My relationship with Karl had been built on a whirlwind courtship. I loved his dashing style and devil-may-care attitude. He was my romantic lead, my special prince.

After we were wed, many of the characteristics which had so attracted me to him became weak links in our combined business enterprises.

I was even more determined to make the marriage succeed when Peter and Kimberli were born. Finally, when my children were 5 and 3, an uncrossable breach occurred. I sued for divorce. It was uncontested. Officially, our marriage existed for fourteen years. Unofficially, it was doomed from the beginning.

After the divorce, I worked even harder to help other people enter into marriages that would last. My methods worked, at least for others.

I determined to be the best possible mother *and* father for my children. I had them christened as infants and later sent them to excellent parochial schools in San Antonio. On weekends when they were home from school, we attended mass together, and on the alternate weekends when they stayed in San Antonio, I traveled to attend church with them.

Truthfully, I only went with them to church because I wanted to set a good example for them. I hardly considered myself the "religious" type, even though I had made that decision in the Iowa country church when I was a child.

I had seen too many other people playing games with religion, going through empty exercises as I had done. Sometimes I wondered, "Did others, too, long for something more with God?" I just didn't know how to make something like that happen. There were seemingly no formulas to follow.

But I couldn't do anything unless I felt I was doing 100 percent. I didn't like just going through the motions.

In fact, one day while kneeling in church with Peter and Kimberli, I confessed, "God! I'm a hypocrite. I've listened to my children pray to you, but I can't talk to You like they can. Please give me their kind of faith — blind faith."

Although I asked God for blind faith, I did not realize at that moment He *did* grant that wish for me. In doing so, He was preparing me to handle the strange series of events that would eventually lead me through a most shadowy valley. Yes, true to my request for Jesus to come into my heart and take over my life at the age of 5, He, indeed had His hand on my life with the Holy Spirit guiding me — way back then. At this time I did not know Jeremiah 33:3 which says, "Call on me and I will answer thee, and shew thee great and mighty things, which thou knowest not." But He honored the blind faith request.

During the winter of 1966, Peter — by then a teenager — was "skiing" along an icy road on his slick-soled cordovan shoes while holding onto the rear bumper of an automobile. Suddenly he was pulled under the vehicle. His legs were seriously injured. He spent four horrible hours in surgery while doctors labored to repair the physical damage. There was speculation that he might even lose his legs. My son needed me as he had never needed me before. Likewise, I prayed for him more diligently than before. It wasn't a major commitment, really, but merely a step in the right direction.

Staying with Peter every night at the hospital, then working overtime in the office was quite an ordeal. When he was released after a month, I was probably the most thankful of all, and I threw a big party to celebrate his homecoming.

I didn't have long to celebrate, however. The morning after Peter's party I awoke with stomach cramps and a terrible pain in my ribs. I was rushed to the same hospital in which Peter had stayed. That was December 22, 1966.

After a series of Xrays and tests, a tentative diagnosis of gastric cancer was made. I was referred to the famed M.D. Anderson Cancer Research Clinic where a group of expert physicians performed a gastroscopic examination and photographed the inner regions of my stomach.

The tight-lipped doctors faced me with my "sentence" — "You have six cancers!" One of them pointed to the vivid color pictures. "If you allow us to remove your stomach, you might live three months. Otherwise, we can't guarantee you another day."

Illness was a totally new experience for me. My father didn't allow malingering among his twelve children, and he fed all of us on the finest farm products to keep us healthy. None of us had ever been seriously ill or even had a broken bone. Furthermore, I had absorbed enough religious training in my childhood to believe all good things come from God, all bad things from Satan.

There arose up in me a ferocious indignation against the devil who was causing the cancers and against the doctors who, for all their technical skills, seemed so ineffective against this evil — almost like robots in their *acceptance* of the enemy's actions. The only real resistance they could offer was to mutilate my body with surgery that would, at least, give me only a few more months of life.

"Your training as surgeons is to cut things out of bodies!" I shouted. "Well, I'm mad at the devil, and I'm not going to let you do it! I'm going to heaven intact."

It's amazing what passes through a human's mind during such horrible, shattering moments. A scripture I had heard as a child flashed into my mind: "Resist the devil, and he will flee from you," (James 4:7).

With that promise surging through my consciousness, I slammed the door of the consultation room and ran to the nearest exit from the building. As I raced across the lawn on the way to my car, I was knocked flat by some unseen force.

No, I hadn't stumbled. Though the sky was cloudless, I thought I had seen lightning.

I'm not certain how long I lay on the ground oblivious of everything around me. When I became aware once more of my surroundings, I got up, brushed myself off, climbed into my car, and drove home. Feeling absolutely famished, I cooked a big dinner and ate it. Afterward, I refused to give any further thought to the cancer and began eating anything I wanted.

Before a month passed, the clinic called and urged me to come in to let the doctors check on the progress of my malignancies. This time, the gastroscope showed

NATIONAL WESTERN LIFE INSURANCE COMPANY   DISABILITY
P.P.BOX 1029
Austin Texas 78767

MAILED TO:

    MRS. PETTI WAGNER   # 64467
    %Maritronics, Inc.
    1400 South Post Oak Road, Suite #2
    Houston, Texas

    From December 16, 1966 until this date Feb 21, 1967
    there has been a remarkable and miraculous healing.

    The first diagnosis from SPRING BRANCH HOSPITAL
    pathology department and our Gastroscopic Examination
    showed much inflammation and <u>six</u> areas of gastric
    ulcerations, carcinomatous type.

    The ulcerations previously seen have healed completely.
    In the region of the one ulcer noted on the last
    examination, Jan, 12, 1967, there is no evidence of
    inflammation. Body and fundus were inspected carefully
    and these are negative as well.

    Impression: Nagative gatroscopy. Complete Healing of
    Cancerous tissue and all gastric ulcerations.

    Dec 16, 20, 21 & 28,1966: Jan 12 &25,1967

GASTROSCOPIES: Jan 12 & 25 1967
GASTROSCOPIES:Dec 16 & 20 1966

        21st   February 67

                M.D. ANDERSON HOSPITAL & TUMOR INSTITUTE
                6723 Bertner Drive, Houston, Texas

FROM:

THE UNIVERSITY OF TEXAS SYSTEM CANCER CENTER
M. D. Anderson Hospital & Tumor Institute
Texas Medical Center, Houston, Texas 77030

TO: *Dr. Petti Wagner*

THE UNIVERSITY OF TEXAS

M. D. ANDERSON HOSPITAL AND TUMOR INSTITUTE

FOLLOW-UP AND PROGRESS NOTES

```
WAGNER MRS O. PETTI          64467-S
PETTI AFDIV 10-30-21         CATH
1400 SO POST OAK RD HOUSTON TEXAS
44467-S    12-16-66          BI-
```

THE UNIVERSITY OF TEXAS
M. D. ANDERSON HOSPITAL AND TUMOR INSTITUTE

REGISTRATION RECORD

z BI-

```
WAGNER MRS O. PETTI          64467-S
PETTI AFDIV 10-30-21         CATH
1400 SO POS OAK RD HOUSTON TEXAS
64467-S    12-16-66          BI-
```

LAST NAME	FIRST	MIDDLE	VETERAN	UNIT NO.	DATE
Wagner,	Mrs.(Olive) Petti		No	64467-S	12/16/66

LEGAL RESIDENCE		COUNTY	MILES FROM	HOW LONG THERE	TEL. NO.
1400 South Post Oak Road, Houston, Texas		Harris		6 yrs	NA 1 0086

AGE	DATE OF BIRTH	PLACE OF BIRTH	RACE	SEX	M S W D SEP.	RELIGION
		Iowa	White	Female		

OCCUPATION (IF RETIRED OR UNEMPLOYED, GIVE FORMER OCCUPATION)	EMPLOYER	ADDRESS
President of Corp.-- Maritronics Inc.		

HOUSTON ADDRESS			TEL. NO.
NEAREST RELATIVE	RELATIONSHIP	ADDRESS	TEL. NO.
NOTIFY IN CASE OF EMERGENCY	RELATIONSHIP	ADDRESS	TEL. NO.

REFERRING PHYSICIAN	ADDRESS	REFERRED DIAGNOSIS	CLINIC
Dr. J.O. McGuire, M.D. 2701 Berry Rd., Houston, Texas		6 Cancer Stomach	S/F Gastro Cl.

AUTHORIZATIONS
RECORD RELEASE

DATE 12/16/66

THE UNIVERSITY OF TEXAS M. D. ANDERSON HOSPITAL AND TUMOR INSTITUTE IS HEREBY AUTHORIZED TO FURNISH THE FOLLOWING NAM
AGENCIES, COMPANIES OR PERSONS ANY OR ALL INFORMATION RELATIVE TO THE CONDITIONS, FINDINGS, DIAGNOSIS, TREATMENT AND PRO

Dr. Nelson at 6 pm

Jan-25-67   GASTROSCOPIC EXAMINATION:
The GTF fiberscope was passed to the level of the antrum. Excellent waves began
immediately to progress on through the pylorus. The antrum and pylorus can be
visualized 100 %. The ulcerations previously seen have healed completely. In
the region of the one ulcer noted on the last examination, there is a single
hemorrhagic spot, but there is no crater or evidence of inflammation. Body and
fundus were inspected carefully and these are negative as well.

Impression: Negative gastroscopy. Complete healing of all gastric ulcerations.

R.S.Nelson,M.D.:ose

SPRING BRANCH MEMORIAL HOSPITAL

8850 LONGPOINT • P.O. BOX 5227 • HOUSTON, TEXAS 77055 • 713-467-6555

September 1?, 198?

Dr Olive P. Warner
2223 Dorrington
Houston, Tex s 77030

Dear Dr. Warner,

According to our Master Patient Card File, you were treated here at Spring

Branch Memorial Hospital in December of 1966.

The Diagnosis was Six Cancers of the Stomach.

Your files were forwarded to M. D. Anderson Research Clinic. You were

transferred to the care of Dr. John Maguire .

Since by law we do not retain copies more than ten years in this office,

This should verify the diagnosis and help them to identify the files.

Sincerely,

Medical Records Dept.

a perfectly healthy stomach. Where there had been six big cancers, there was not even a trace of scar tissue!

The registration records listed in the University of Texas System Cancer Center (M.D. Anderson Hospital and Tumor Institute) and the records for the National Western Life Insurance Company all point to one basic fact: There was a complete healing of cancerous tissue and all gastric ulcerations.

Why? Good grief — I didn't know. I didn't know any spiritual significance of my fall to the ground. It was just obvious that a miracle of healing had taken place in my body. I just thought it was a simple case of "Whatever will be, will be." Some people were meant to be religious. Some had a talent for making money. Sometimes miracles happened. I was just glad to be alive, thankful to be back working.

And if that wasn't enough, a year later I received another strange, supernatural signal. I began to lose my voice. Then, it was still quite chic to smoke. My own favorite brand was the long green Pall Mall cigarettes. During 1967, however, my voice became so weak that I was forced to communicate by using a notepad and pencil. Four months went by. I consulted several doctors. Each gave the same diagnosis: cancer of the throat and larynx, and precancerous laukoplakia on the vocal cords.

During the time a physician friend recommended that I see a Houston ear, nose, and throat specialist.

When I was first ushered into his office, I was strangely comfortable and drawn. Scripture quotations hung on his walls. In his waiting room, I found Bibles with certain passages outlined. Then he prayed for me before performing a laryngascopy and taking a specimen for biopsy. I thought him to be awfully religious, but I liked something about him — something I couldn't quite explain. I trusted him.

When the biopsy report arrived, the doctor diagnosis was the same as that given by the other doctors with whom I had consulted. The doctor recommended immediate surgery.

That time I didn't resist. Somehow I felt safe in his hands, confident I could trust him to do only what was absolutely necessary.

However, the next day, as I was being wheeled through the hospital corridor toward the operating room, my voice suddenly returned! After all those months of silence, I was able to speak without so much of a rasp!

I talked to the nurse. She and the orderly practically ran to the operating room where the doctor was waiting. He was astonished. He had this curious, knowing smile.

Instead of proceeding with the anesthetic, he quickly reexamined me. There was no trace of disease. The cancer *and* the leukoplakia had completely disappeared!

"There's no medical explanation for this," the doctor said, continuing to flash that grin. "But I know a miracle when I see one."

Once more, I had been delivered safely out of danger. My life had been given back to me. I felt fortunate, of course, but though I was thankful to be alive, it didn't bring any major change.

Life was more precious to me, but I just wanted things to get back to normal.

CHAPTER 5

All That Glitters

Wealth has different effects on different people. Even though I had carved out my own empire, I had come from money, so I had few of the problems the *nouveaux riches* face — the insecurities, the overindulgences, the brazenness. Also, I had few of the manipulative characteristics of those born rich. I had my name in the Social Register; yet, I always realized that did not make me a dime.

To me, having money merely meant being flexible to invest, to develop, to (quite frankly) make more money. If anything, I worked harder as my wealth grew. It wasn't some fear-of-losing-everything obsession; instead, I truly loved helping people. Even as a child, I had always been a giving person. That hadn't changed even though I had developed four multimillion dollar corporations.

By 1970, however, carving out that empire had gotten to be a round-the-clock job. Although I had sold my interest in three corporations — Niamco (therapeutic equipment), Herbagere (hydroponic grass-growing machines), and Menotti (cold-wave permanents) — I still owned five buildings on a block in one of Houston's nicer areas. One of the buildings, 4500 sq. ft., contained my penthouse apartment, my Maritronics offices, and a kitchen which fed five hundred people taking part (at that time) in a double-blind study in the field of diet control. In the next block, I also owned a large medical clinic doing double-blind studies for five major drug companies which were seeking to obtain new drug labeling from the FDA.

A fourth of my day was spent in supervising the medical projects. The rest of the time, I worked on furthering my long-term pet endeavor — Maritronics International. After 23 years, Maritronics had been responsible for more than 150,000 marriages, only seven of which were known to have ended in divorce. During that same period of time, Houston had plunged from its unenviable position as the city with the highest divorce rate to fifteenth place in the country.

At 55, I could look back with much pleasure. All along I had believed that if I helped enough people get what they wanted, then I would also be blessed. All my projects were continuing to succeed, and everything in my life seemed to be running smoothly.

I enjoyed my work immensely, but it left me virtually no time to relax. A lifetime of overwork began to take its toll.

Quite frankly, I felt I deserved a rest. Both of my children were in school (Kimberli in San Antonio, and I had enrolled Peter in Houston's St. Thomas University). Even in the midst of my career as a businesswoman, I had always spent as much time as possible with my two children.

But I wanted to start enjoying life for myself. Retirement began to sound appealing. I decided, over a period of time, to start streamlining my interests, to reduce my responsibilities so that I could dust off my golf clubs. I wanted to play the horses more, to travel without so many time restrictions, to sip drinks beside the pool in lazy country club afternoons.

As I set my sights on semi-retiring, I also started to distribute some of my assets. Through several well-known friends, I was able to make college scholarships available. Eventually, those grants helped four hundred students in different prestigious schools. It wasn't something I did to boost my ego, but what I relished doing merely to help young people.

I had also made provisions for Peter and Kimberli to receive the pre-planned inheritance to start their own business enterprises after they graduated.

Once I had made that decision to semi-retire, my mind exploded with creative thoughts. Happy memories surfaced of the times in my life when I had been less driven, when I had excelled at such things as golf.

I couldn't have asked for more. Everything was going well — my business, my personal life, my plans. Everything.

"Then why," I asked myself, "do I feel such a vague uneasiness about my business affairs?" Something mysterious, indefinable, almost ominous seemed fomenting in the undercurrent.

"It's only my imagination," I tried to convince myself. "It's just that I've been working even more overtime since I've made up my mind to retire."

Yet, I knew it had to be more than that. To be honest, I had been less and less involved with the "nuts and bolts" of my business. Of my employees in the medical clinic, I mainly came in contact with the nurses, five doctors, psychologist, and research head. I spent half my day there, but I had delegated most of the administrative responsibilities to Zelda, my assistant.

Then, I normally spent the other half of my day in my

Maritronics Corporation office, concentrating on the giant task of helping people and counseling soon-to-be-married couples.

Despite being busily involved with the counseling and research, I had, nevertheless, noticed a rapid, inexplicable turnover among the office workers on my staff — the people who worked closely with Zelda.

The accountant who had been with me 15 years had suddenly left without a word to me — just moved away to another state, or so Zelda and his brother related.

Other trusted employees had been leaving, too. In fact, the turnover had reached 16 within the last months of 1970. One by one, however, they were replaced by new personnel sent by an employment agency about which I knew nothing. The agency contacted Zelda each time; she helped screen the new workers and came with glowing reports about certain ones.

It was especially disturbing that my offices had experienced such turnover, since I wanted to reduce my energies expended toward running my businesses. I hardly wanted to be involved in training new people. Thankfully, Zelda helped in that account, too.

Deep down, I sensed something was very wrong. What was it? I couldn't figure it out.

I just figured that if there was any reason to be suspicious about anything, Zelda would have to know.

Zelda had come to me highly recommended during 1970. She was an ideal adminstrative assistant, as I soon found out. She was pleasant, in her mid-forties, had an attractive figure and blue eyes. Underneath, however, there was a hardness. She didn't have a real compassion for all the people with whom we worked. But what she lacked in understanding, she redeemed herself with hard, dedicated work. She definitely lived up to her credentials. From her curly red hair to her stylish shoes, she was the epitome of an administrator.

During the first three months she was with me, Zelda really took a load off my shoulders. She always followed through with little details, so I put her increasingly in charge. She even got Peter enrolled in college and encouraged him to get his own "pad" (I let him use one of my apartments).

She was a calm whirlwind, making things run smoothly in my business and home. When I started a new research program with 500 diet volunteers, she was more than willing to make sure that I was fed a similar menu from our large kitchen that was a part of the office complex. Little touches like that made her a valuable employee, especially since I could turn even more of my attention to making the transition toward curtailing my business interests.

I even let Zelda write out all my checks — everything but signing them — and keep me posted on all accounting matters. As mentioned before, she was invaluable to me.

And since she was such a trusted and capable employee, I felt sure she would have called my attention to anything seriously wrong in the businesses. It didn't relieve the nagging feeling, however. I kept wavering back and forth between confidence and doubt.

I made Zelda manager of my medical clinic, just two doors up the street from my Maritronics operation. With her heavy responsibilities went additional salary and authority. I felt like I could count on her for anything.

She was a whiz with the clinic. Each day the participants in the diet-control study came in to be weighed, to have vital signs and mood scales tabulated, to have blood pressure checked, and to pick up two styrofoam containers holding that day's food supply.

Zelda was so thoughtful. Before the diet-kitchen employees left for the Christmas holidays, she had extra meals prepared for me and stored in my freezer at home so that I would not be troubled with the necessity of meal preparation. That was typical of her concern about small details.

Truthfully, I wasn't pleased with the meals I had been receiving from the kitchen. I felt I should participate in the program, but it had seemed to me that all my food tasted peculiar — as if it had meat tenderizer in it. When I asked Zelda to look into the matter, she reported back to me that the flavor was simply the special blend of spices used in the diet.

"You will get used to it in time," she assured me.

Before the Christmas season, I felt increasingly sluggish. However, with holiday activities — dining with friends and going to parties — I became so caught up in festivities that I didn't bother to follow the clinic diet. It seemed strange to me, but in spite of my irregular holiday eating patterns, I felt considerably better. I threw Zelda's frozen meals into the garbage.

After New Year's Day, the employees returned, and our diet kitchen reopened. Zelda began seeing that I got the freshly-cooked, diet meals again. Almost immediately I became aware of my pre-holiday symptoms — nausea and a viselike squeezing sensation on my chest — which were impossible to ignore.

Those symptoms became so severe on Saturday, March 6, that I went to see Dr. McGuire, a dear friend to whom I had once been engaged. He treated me for food poisoning, gave me a friendly take-care-of-yourself lecture, prescribed plenty of rest, and sent me home.

The nagging apprehension remained that something was very, very wrong, but I kept trying to talk myself out of that fear, thinking that I was overtired.

It was early 1971 when I received a disturbing letter from the relative of a close friend:

Petti,

Something is going to happen to you during the next few months, but don't worry — everything is going to come out all right eventually.

God has me doing intercessory prayer for you. Do you remember several years ago when you were in the hospital and a specialist was going to take out your larynx? You had cancer of the throat and had not talked for months. God sent me to Houston to pray for you . . .

Well, God is having me pray for you ...

I never met the writer who penned the letter, but I understood from my friend that she was involved in some peculiar religious pursuits. I had run into some of those "holy rollers," as we called them in Iowa, when I was a teenager (during a service, two women had taken me to a back room and prayed over me in a strange sounding language). Looking back, I began to realize my "fortunate" string of successes had started when those two women prayed over me, but I had felt so uncomfortable. The writer of the letter made me feel the same way. It was hard for me to comprehend the purpose of her brief message. Was it encouragement? Was it a warning? Was she going to come to Houston again to pray for me? Whatever it was, the letter was so strange that I dismissed it from my mind.

Even though I felt like something was wrong, there was little reason to be suspicious of anything. Everything was going too well. I was on top of the world, business-wise, and with my upcoming retirement, I was facing the most glorious years of my life.

Sunday, March 7, 1971, would have been an exquisite day for golf and brunch at Ruby's. Ruby and her husband John were dear friends who always had open house around their pool on Sundays. It was one of my favorite places to go. There was always spicy conversation, laughter, and occasional well-known faces dropping in. Ordinarily, I'd have gone there that day.

Instead, I decided to go to the seven o'clock Mass at

St. Vincent DePaul. I had never done this on my own. I only went when my children were home, since it was a routine I wanted them to continue.

Yet, there I was, alone, wanting to pray for the first time in many years. I didn't really know how to begin, and I certainly didn't think I was entitled to expect any results. I mean, despite the fact that I had a giving heart and had helped many people, I wasn't religious. However, praying seemed to be the thing to do, especially since I felt so uneasy about the insidious undercurrent or whatever-it-was at work.

"Lord," I said. My words sounded dry and mechanical — "I feel like there is something wrong, something horrible trying to take hold of my life. I don't know what it is. Please send me Your help."

The words weren't very spiritual sounding. At least, I didn't think they were. It was the best I could manage. I just hoped the prayer got through.

I rose from my knees and left the church. When I reached the street, someone in a passing car waved to me, then pulled over to the curb. It was Lana, a young woman who had worked for me four years earlier as a clerk and administrative assistant. She had been forced to resign when her invalid mother had come to live with her. Her mother had since passed away, and she was just getting off her 11-7 shift at the Ben Taub County Hospital.

I wondered if Lana was an answer to my prayer, and I decided to confide in her.

"Do me a favor," I said. "Come over to the office tomorrow about two o'clock and stay until closing time. Something peculiar is going on. Keep your eyes open and see if you can discover what it is — or if you think it's only my imagination. We can have dinner afterward and talk about it."

When Lana readily accepted my invitation, I knew that God had heard my call for help.

As promised, Lana came in the next day. She was still there when the telephone call came about my Aunt Anna, about the heart attack, about the Southwest General Hospital.

"Don't leave until I get back," I yelled, rushing toward my car.

But Lana and I would never talk about what was going on in my office. We would never share that late dinner.

My comfortable, wonderful, rewarding world was about to be shattered into a living hell.

CHAPTER 6

Shadowy Valley

Back at my office, Zelda was closing up for the day. Seeing Lana, she asked, "What are *you* still doing here?"

"Waiting for Dr. Wagner to get back," Lana answered.

"Oh, Dr. Wagner won't be back tonight. I just talked with her. She's been called away to take care of some urgent business."

"But what about her aunt?"

"It's okay," Zelda replied calmly. "That was a false alarm. Her Aunt Anna is going to be fine. You might as well go on home."

"But Dr. Wagner would have called me, I'm sure," Lana insisted. "She knows I'm waiting for her."

Zelda shrugged. "I'm sorry. I'm only telling you what she told me. That's all I know to tell you."

Lana knew that I had been suspicious about something in my office. Perhaps that's why, without telling Zelda, Lana left the office, got into her car, and headed straight for Southwest General Hospital. When she arrived, she didn't see my car in the parking lot, but she went inside the mostly deserted building. She apparently ran into the same nurse who had given me the injection.

"I'm looking for Anna Carnes' room," Lana inquired. "Do you know what room she's in?"

"Carnes? There's no one here by that name."

Lana was perplexed. "But there must be. The hospital called my friend, Dr. Wagner, and said her aunt was going to be admitted because of a heart attack."

Lana didn't give up easily. She kept asking questions. Once, the nurse said that I was a patient under Dr. Ronald Holmes' authority (a notorious doctor who had been implicated in the Artesia Hall scandal for authorizing antiquated electroshock treatments which had irreversibly damaged the minds of many patients). But when Lana phoned Dr. McGuire, who had been personal doctor for both of us for years, the same nurse denied to him that anyone named Carnes or Wagner were there.

Still, the nurse aroused Lana's suspicions. Lana, in turn, appealed to Dr. McGuire. He came over to check out the situation for himself. He came several times, in fact. He presented himself as my doctor. He even persuaded the police to accompany him on one occasion. Each time the hospital staff denied my presence.

Upstairs, inside a crayon-inscribed Room 120, I went through the worst possible torture. Day after day.

When I regained consciousness, my first thought was of the big feet of those two sadistic men. I remembered the boots smashing into my skull and mouth, jackhammers pounding at me with an incessant rhythmic force. I shuddered uncontrollably in the deadly silence enveloping the room.

More than anything, one thought ran over and over through my groggy brain — "How can this be happening to me? How?"

As the room stopped spinning so violently, I realized that I was only seeing with my right eye. Instinctively, though with great effort, I lifted my right hand to my face. The slightest touch sent waves of agony coursing through my body.

"Oh, God!" I could feel my left eyeball protruding so far from its socket that I couldn't even open the lid over it.

My jaw was smashed and swelling. Pieces of torn flesh hung from my fingers.

"My face! Oh, God — what have they done to me?"

Frantically, I felt myself. All I could feel were painful bumps. My hands smeared the sticky ooze of blood.

I groped gingerly around me for my purse. I wanted to get tissues to wipe the blood from my face. Just that minimal motion sent further torturous throbs through me. My shoulder felt pulled from its socket.

Groping, I touched nothing on the gritty floor which resembled my purse. As my eye became accustomed to the darkness, and in the dim light from a flashing time-and-temperature sign across the street from the hospital, I could make out the dark outlines of a bed and nightstand in the otherwise bare room. There was no purse anywhere.

The pain shooting from my fingers forced me to look at my hands.

"Not my rings, too!"

All my beautiful rings were missing, all — that is — except for a new honor ring Tiffany's had completed for me a few days previously. They had soldered it on my finger. The diamonds to that ring had come from various pins and rings and lockets which had been presented to me for service and achievements in the various fields of endeavor. In many ways, that ring represented my entire life, but it was crusted with a burgundy-colored liquid. It was cutting into my torn and bleeding finger, swollen by then like a sausage.

Then I remembered, but I wasn't sure when, that I had regained consciousness momentarily, and I felt the guards savagely jerking rings from my fingers. Before I had collapsed unconscious again, I recalled my horror as they cursed and pried with something like a dull kitchen knife, trying to get off the tighter fitting rings. Obviously, they hadn't succeeded with the honor ring.

I gingerly touched my neck and wrist, knowing already what I would find. All my other elegant jewelry, a watch and several necklaces, were missing. I knew I had lost a fortune.

"Perhaps that's why they did all this." But I couldn't figure out how they would have called me about Aunt Anna. It still didn't make sense.

"How can this be happening to me?"

But I didn't want to think about the jewelry. I was shiveringly cold. My brain was still muddled from the drugs they had injected. My left eye was useless, and my right eye kept refusing to focus.

Trembling, I clung desperately to consciousness. Something drove me to drag myself over to the dilapidated old bed. It took everything I could muster to pull myself up onto it.

I tried to wipe the still-caking blood from my mouth and teeth and face with a corner of the sheet.

"If only I had some water and a washcloth!" Curious — the thoughts that run through the human mind during the worst, hellish moments. Although the inside of my mouth was too raw for me to use a toothbrush, I kept thinking how tingling clean toothpaste might have done away with the awful, rusty, bloody taste in my mouth.

I lay there some time trying to survey my surroundings, to assess the situation.

When I could get my right eye to work, I saw evidence

that I was imprisoned in a room obviously not used for some time. The walls were cracked and dingy. The flashing light from across the street was reflected on chipped and flaking paint, on cobwebbed ceiling corners. The lone door had a single window, just higher than my head. On the outside wall, three barred windows were covered with one huge, thick sheet of Plexiglas. Between the Plexiglas and the bars were smaller panes of glass.

Even if I could have screamed at that moment, no one could have heard me outside my third story window.

I felt paralyzed with unbelievable horror. I was completely alone, horribly battered, locked in a musty, foul-smelling room. There was no means of escape.

The air reeked of stale urine. That stench, mixed with the odor of my own drying blood, sent waves of nausea washing over me again. I fell into a semi-conscious delirium.

Half asleep, I ached for sunrise to come and banish this whole nightmarish scene. Someone — Zelda or Lana or maybe Dr. McGuire — someone would surely rescue me. Surely.

But it was not to be.

After an agonizing eternity, actually just a few hours, the skinny nurse came back. She flipped on a flickering florescent light. Before I could react, she jabbed me again through the sleeve of my blouse with a hypodermic needle. I was still too battered, too shattered to resist.

"Is ... is that some ... kind of ... painkiller?" I mumbled dully. "Because if it is... I'm allergic to medication ... I can't even take an aspirin."

"Hell no," she snarled, "it's just something to keep you quiet so you won't be screaming for help."

Her eyes narrowed, but she merely glared for a moment, then left the room. Soon the sedation brought the merciful blackness again.

Some time later I awoke. I noticed daylight streaming through the windows. I also noticed, for the first time, that the Plexiglas *and* the outer window panes were held in place with many Phillips screws. Maybe hundreds of them.

The door opened, and a petite young Black nurse's aide entered. She wore a blue-check uniform, and tiptoed in carrying a breakfast tray. Without a word, she put the tray down on the nightstand and fled. Small wonder. At first I thought she was afraid of me — that maybe she thought I was a dangerous mental patient. Then I saw the reason for her fright — Steel-and-Thunder was standing guard outside my door. As the aide passed by him, he banged the door shut. I heard the dead-bolt click into place, just like the night before.

The mere sight of food made my stomach retch. My teeth were loose and my gums badly damaged. But I knew I had to keep my strength up — for whatever was ahead. Finally, after considering the tray for a few moments, I tentatively decided to try to eat.

There was a small carton of milk. I opened it, despite the bursting pain from my mangled knuckles, and poured the white liquid onto a bowl of cooked cereal.

When I maneuvered the spoon through my puffy lips, the first bite brought a horrible, sickening realization. There was a vaguely familiar taste — coppery, like meat tenderizer — just like I tasted in the diet meals Zelda had brought me. It hit me like a thunderbolt.

Looking down, I saw a tiny perforation near the top of the milk carton. Perhaps it was just my imagination, but it certainly looked like a needle had pierced the carton.

"Poison?" It seemed too outlandish to even consider. "Someone has been trying to poison me — maybe even kill me! But why? Why are they? Who are they?"

My trembling questions hung in the stagnant air like smoky taunts.

The dearth of noise and activity around me on the third floor led me to believe that I must be the only patient on it.

I forced myself to get up. Thankfully, I realized that — despite the beating — I had no broken bones. I was stiff. Each step tormented my brain. I looked past the glass. The sparse number of cars in the parking lot hardly indicated a thriving business for the hospital. I noticed that my white Cadillac convertible was missing. The keys, my car, my purse with all the credit cards — everything kept adding up to an increasingly traumatic total.

"But why are they holding me hostage here — in this room?"

I spent the day crossing the line of consciousness — back and forth, back and forth. The sedation had a strange effect upon me.

The room became an eerie setting for a continuing nightmare of unthinkable horrors. There seemed to be no escape, no reprieve, no hope.

Later on the second evening of my imprisonment, Steel-and-Thunder and the Follower burst through the door, grabbed me by my dark hair, and one of them shone a powerful flashlight into my face — point-blank. This new violence became a sporadic part of my torture. I became terrified to risk the oblivion of sleep until I could no longer keep awake.

The open wounds and bruised parts of my body needed immediate care, especially my horribly injured eye, but I had no way to treat myself. I had no water. There was no bathtub, not even a sink. There were no toilet facilities.

Because I had never taken strong medication, the injections and drugged food gave me severe diarrhea. I tried to get the guards to let me use a toilet, but there was no response from outside my door. The cramps doubled me up, and finally I had no choice but to use a corner of the room.

That was the most revolting thing I ever had to do in my life. I had always been an extremely fastidious, meticulous person — maybe to a fault. But all my pride was demolished in the humiliation of being forced to relieve myself on the floor in the corner of that already-smelly room.

"Oh God, this can't be happening to me. Why doesn't somebody come to help me?"

But there would be no help — just more horrors. An acute allergic reaction to the drugs caused terrible itching hives. I determined, no matter how hungry I got, that I couldn't risk eating any more food, unless there was bread or a hard roll that looked safe.

There were more beatings. At first, when Steel-and-Thunder and his Follower came into my room, I fought. I didn't know if they were going to rape me, or kill me, or what.

My father had taught his girls that one well-placed kick — "Hit him were he lives!" he had said — would foil any man who gave us trouble.

So I fought, but in spite of my violent screaming, kicking, and clawing, I was helpless against the two men. They were obviously used to working with unco-operative mental patients. They had a leather-covered paddle which one of them often used to pummel my back and hips and legs.

Each whack sent another searing, humiliating reminder through my body that they were in control, that I had no rights anymore, that there might never be an end to the abyss in which I was rapidly plunging.

After each brutal beating, many times after being securely spread-eagled with belting to the four corners of the bed, I would feel the blackness sweeping over me. I truly believed death was coming. And I didn't care anymore.

But I always awakened again, after a time, to find myself in the familiar, fiendish room.

During those hours and days, I kept searching my mind, wondering who could be behind such a horrible torture. I had no enemies — none that I knew of.

"Why is this happening to me?"

After the first day passed, then the second, I realized that robbery couldn't have been the only motive. They hadn't killed me, even after they got all my jewelry and purse (with the $3000 dollars worth of receipts from Maritronics) and credit cards and Cadillac.

No. It had to be more. Perhaps I had been kidnapped for a ransom. That was strange, though, especially if it had been engineered by anyone who knew me well. Even though I was an heiress of the Peet family fortune, long before my parents died, that money had been placed in trusts, invested, and spent. Anyone who was relatively close to me (close enough, at least, to set a trap using Aunt Anna's name), would know that I had few liquid funds available. Everything I had was tied up somewhere making more money. I had Haskins and Sells seeing to that. All my family was pretty much the same.

"It has to be something besides kidnapping. But what?"

Before long, my physical strength began to lapse. Dehydration followed. I was permitted no water for washing and was given drinking water only for swallowing the large pills they started forcing on me several times a day. I recognized what they were immediately — lithium tablets, sometimes used in the treatment of manic-depressive patients. I knew what devastating effects they could have on a normal individual, so I knew I couldn't swallow a single one.

That wasn't easy. When it was time for another pill several times a day, at least one of the guards would come in with Skinny, the nurse, and would force a tablet into my mouth. Then, like one would force a dog, they would pour water in my mouth and rub my throat to make me swallow the medication.

From the very first time, however, I was able to conceal the lithium capsule underneath my tongue and hold it in place while I swallowed the water down my parched throat. Then, when my gloating captors would leave the room, I would spit the pill out and hide it under the mattress. Since my bed linens were never changed, that was obviously a good place. I wanted to be able to take the pills with me for proof of the fiendish treatment when (and if) I ever got out of Room 120.

They continued the sadistic injections, too. During the brief periods when the drugs wore off, I calculated that they were attempting to make me swallow 6000 milligrams of lithium each day! From counseling many different types of psychiatric patients, I knew that even extremely manic personalities could only tolerate 300-600 milligrams of lithium per day.

The drugs, the coppery taste in my food (just like in those diet meals Zelda had brought to me), the knowledge about Aunt Anna — everything seemed to point to a connection somehow with the strange things which had been happening in my office.

"But Zelda would have known. She would have told me. I'm sure."

I asked, but my captors — during their sporadic forays into the room — refused to talk. I got no hints as to what it was all about, just pain. When I asked anything, the beatings were more savage.

In the midst of my *gehenna*, only the Black girl who brought my food seemed to have any feelings of compassion for me ("Jane" — I read on her nametag).

One morning when she entered my room to deliver the breakfast tray, she looked straight into my bruised face and whispered, "Is there any way I can help you, ma'am?"

I groped for an answer as she glanced apprehensively over her shoulder to see if anyone had heard her. She seemed innocent, like I could trust her.

"Jane," the whispered words flowed from my cracked and still-puffy mouth, "if you'll take a message to my friend, Judge Carl Walker, in downtown Houston, I'll give you a million dollars!"

I knew what I said was wrong even before I finished. Her eyes were large as saucers. She was terrified — "Ma'am, I'm scared of what these men would do to me if they caught me running off with a note to your judge."

Too late, I realized that the large sum was too unbelievable (even if I didn't have the liquid funds, I would have come up with the money somehow if she would have taken the message — I was that desperate and afraid for my life). If I had offered her something smaller, a hundred dollars, something she could comprehend, she might have taken the risk.

She did do something for me, though. She began concealing things for me, a pen and scraps of paper, beneath her uniform and brought them to me. I wanted to document my daily existence, wanting to write down everything done to me, every thought, every emotion, each detail of the physical and psychological horror happening to me.

"If I don't get out of here alive, maybe the notes will serve some purpose. At least someone will know why I disappeared without a trace."

I hid the paper beneath the bed along with the growing mound of lithium tablets.

There was certainly plenty of time for exploration and examination of my sparse surroundings. Even though my brain remained somewhat numbed by the injections, still, there were brief periods when the drugs would wear off. During those times, I memorized every small detail. The room seemed like an impenetrable fortress.

Always, there was at least one guard outside the door. I could hear the scraping of his chair, the clearing of his throat, sometimes even muffled conversation.

Overlooking the street and parking area were those three windows. Each window, upon closer examination, had five iron bars extending down from the top of the frame to the bottom sash. All three windows were covered with a thick wall of Plexiglas (I had noticed that the first night), beginning two feet from the floor and going all the way to the top of the windows. Between the Plexiglas and the bars were the smaller panes of glass. The Plexiglas wall and the smaller sheets of glass were held in place with 200 Phillip's head screws. Not 199, nor 201 — exactly 200. I counted them innumerable times during those days as I tried to keep my mind working, to make myself think about something other than the injections, to force myself to think of a way I could escape. It all seemed so hopeless.

Even in the macabre nightmare, I knew it was vital to maintain contact with reality. Just seeing the time-and-temperature sign across the street brought an almost-euphoric connection with the outside world that otherwise seemed so far away.

And I kept doing as many other practical things as I could think about: repeating my name, my address, my telephone number, particulars about my work. I kept track of the days which passed from the changing daylight and dark outside my windows. I jotted the dates on scraps of paper.

I even counted the diamonds on my honor ring, 58 diamonds still caked with blood. I forced myself to remember where each diamond came from — which award ceremony, but there were many times I couldn't remember much because of the drugs surging through my body. That frustrated me further when I could not make my numbed brain work.

But somehow I kept reaffirming my own identity. I made myself believe that I was still alive. At times I wanted to live more than anything else. Other times, I knew I was unquestionably going to die.

Hour after jagged hour stretched on as the surrealistic nightmare swept around me — the beatings, injections, Jane's innocent face, Steel-and-Thunder, the Follower, Skinny, Roger (a young man who alternated with Jane in bringing me trays of the tainted food — he looked so frightened when I asked him to help me). I wondered sometimes if I were losing my grip on reality. It was tormentingly difficult to keep things in perspective as the injections sent me into a spinning, torpid, black abyss.

On the eighth day, my torture was increased. Skinny snarled, "We're giving you lithium so the authorities will find the drug in your bloodstream."

"What authorities?" I cried. "Who are you working with? Why is this happening to me?"

No explanation.

And I remember the beating that day more than the rest. When the two guards came into the room, Steel-and-Thunder, always the spokesman, growled, "Lady, today we're gonna break your spirit. Nobody cares about you. Nobody's interested in what's happening to you. And nobody here in the hospital is gonna help you."

I remember that beating most, because I fought harder than ever before. I still had fingernails, and I dug them into any flesh I could reach — scratching and clawing and kicking. Almost like a rag doll, I was slapped to the floor, kicked, and beaten. It was like a game to them. That — more than anything — made my hell even more unfathomable. How could humans treat another human so routinely horribly?

And I recall, above my muffled sobs, Steel-and-Thunder taunted, "Wagner, after we're finished torturing you, then we're gonna dump your bloody body into Galveston Bay and let the fishes eat you like a piece of garbage!"

He was just goading me, I could tell. Or was he?

As I lay on the bed, bleeding from reopened wounds, my right eye only partially open (the left was completely useless), pain charged through every cell of my being. I knew, more than ever before, that I was dying.

Through the door — I don't know if it was shut or open — I heard the Follower laughing viciously: "How much more can that old goat take? How long are we gonna have to rot up here? What's she made out of?"

There was more laughing as the muffled voices became less distinct.

Then, suddenly the room filled with the most loving voice I had ever heard. It was an answer to the guard's questions, but I was the one who heard the words: "She is made of tough fiber."

Those were words my mother would have used! But the voice was not hers. For some reason, I don't remember why, I wondered if it were an angel's voice.

I just know that I had been on the edge, ready to go under, willing to let go, and those loving words were like a fresh lifeline flung out to me. I had been drowning, swallowed up in a sea of hatred and indifference.

But I knew the words were true. My mother had told me the same phrase many times. I *was* made of tough fiber. I had endured so much, but I was still alive.

I was a survivor with a well-above-average will to live. Clinging to those words of encouragement which had been spoken at the precise and perfect moment, I chose to live. That tough fiber, that survival instinct throbbed through my veins.

But I was to learn that, before I could truly live again, I would have to cross into the most unimaginable, unearthly sphere.

I would have to die.

CHAPTER 7

Death Chamber

I was awakened the next morning by the guards. I felt them grabbing my long raven locks and yanking me into an upright position.

"I thought we were through with you last night!" Steel-and-Thunder bellowed. The Follower stared at me in disgust, like he was being blamed for my still being alive.

They held me as Skinny stuck me through my black blouse like so many times before. Then they did something I hardly expected. Suddenly I was dragged out of my prison. Down a hallway they took me, then into a room.

Ice water flashed through my veins when I saw an antiquated electroshock machine.

"Hey!" Steel-and-Thunder gloated, "d'ya know anything about shock treatment?"

My skin crawled. I couldn't make any words come out. I knew I had just been given the death sentence (or worse — to live as a vegetable). I tried to break away, but it was impossible.

"But we ain't gonna give you the usual 170 volts," he rasped. "We're gonna give you all of 'em — 240! That's enough to snuff you out like a candle." His demonic laugh was joined by similar smirks from the other two.

I screamed, but Skinny clamped her hand tight over my mouth, carefully avoiding my splintered teeth. I fought against the waves of venom-like drugs she had injected earlier, and I struggled to get free from the men's viselike grasps.

But I was flung onto a cold steel table, strapped down, stripped to the waist, and felt electrodes being attached to my temples and chest.

In one final, superhuman effort to break free, I writhed and jerked, but the steely giant broad-handed me on the skull. I felt blackness sweeping over me.

"This can't be happening to me!" It was like the most unbelievable scene in a Boris Karloff movie.

I saw Skinny walk quickly to the switch on the wall. The men let me go. I heard a buzz. Immediately the windowless room was pitch black.

But I heard noises. I saw the door opened. There was cursing. I understood.

"Damn electricity went off!" Steel-and-Thunder's voice snapped.

I began sobbing with relief. By some mysterious "mistake," I had been saved from electrocution.

Skinny raged at the men who were already working furiously to get the electricity back on. Their efforts were obviously fruitless. I was unhooked, partially draped, dragged back down the hallway, and thrown headfirst into Room 120.

My head ached from massive shock and the volts which had charged, however briefly, through my terrorized body.

"Why don't you just go ahead and kill me?" I sobbed.

"Get it over with ... but why?"

Sometime during the day, as my right eye focused, I noticed that my hair was no longer black. It had turned, as much as I could see without a mirror to use, to snowy-white. I wondered if such a transformation could take place with electroshock patients. It must be some phenomenon. I still wasn't prepared for what I saw. Would the nightmare ever end?

Apparently I wasn't the only one who observed the startling color change of my hair.

Not long before dark, Roger, the orderly who sometimes brought me food, came into my room with a curly, black wig which was stretched over a Styrofoam wig head. I was totally perplexed.

Roger seemed like Jane, like an innocent participant, so I decided to risk a few questions.

"What's that for?" I asked feebly.

"It's for you to wear."

"But why should I wear such a hideous wig?" I pleaded. "Why won't they give me a comb or brush to dress my own? Can you find my purse for me? A hairbrush?"

He just shook his head, nervously looking over his shoulder at the door like the nurse's aide had done. Still, perhaps out of sympathy, he reached into his pocket and handed me a short black comb.

"Here," he whispered, "you can use this one."

I knew I would have it for just a moment, so I struggled to get the worst tangles in my matted, white hair. Sometimes the strangest things bring the greatest pleasure. It was such a relief just to comb my hair, just to have somebody in my room who didn't seem bent on destroying me.

"There," I breathed, handing the comb back to him, "That looks better, doesn't it?"

He nodded noncommittally, so I pleaded again, "You don't think I need the wig now, do you?"

"Well, no-n-no ma'am," he stammered, continuing to glance over his shoulder. "But Dr. Holmes — h-h-he said he wanted you to be wearing this wig when you are found."

Dr. Holmes? Not THE Dr. Ronald Holmes — the most notorious psychiatrist in Texas!

"Please, God!" I breathed.

In the past, I had counseled with a number of his patients, trying to help them back to health after he had virtually wiped away their minds with excessive shock treatments. He was known as the worst psychiatrist in a state known for its disgraceful medical and mental health standards — standards which allowed a place like Southwest General to continue treating people. In most states, Dr. Holmes would have lost his license, especially after the malpractice suits and the highly-publicized Artesia Hall scandal.

How ironic that I had fallen into the clutches of the very man whose victims I had tried to rehabilitate!

"I have to get out of here! Please," I begged, "They're trying to kill me! Can't you help me? Name your price — I'll pay it."

"I wish I could, lady," he whispered, "but there's no way. I'm being watched more closely than you are, because I've spoken out against their treatment of you. In fact, they're probably counting the time I'm in here with you now. I'd better go, before . . ."

He left abruptly without finishing the sentence. Another chance to escape was gone.

"Oh God!"

I was so weak, it was an effort for me to stay awake. Finally I gave in to the blackness.

It was still night, two days later, when the florescent light came on over my bed. I looked around, but no one was in the room!

I knew what that meant. Terror flooded my heart. Power had been restored to the third floor. My stay of execution had ended.

I had no strength or will to fight left in me when Skinny and the two men came into my room later that morning. I made an effort to resist, but Steel-and-Thunder swung some kind of a blunt instrument at my head. I couldn't see exactly what he used. I just felt the sickening thud.

I watched, dazed, as I was dragged again into the death chamber. They handled me like a limp hunk of meat, throwing me onto the cold steel table, ripping open my clothing, fastening the electrodes in place.

"240?" Skinny demanded.

"It's there!" The Follower answered.

The switch clicked, just like before, but the electricity didn't stop. There was no reprieve. I felt the crackle of current along the wires. My nostrils flared at the smell of singed flesh.

I was drowning, submerged in a hysterical wave of mind-rending jolts.

My body arched spasmodically, then collapsed and lay limp on the table.

STATE OF TEXAS   **CERTIFICATE OF DEATH**   STATE FILE NO

1 NAME OF DECEASED (Type or print)	(a) First CLIVE (b) Middle (c) Last
3 DATE OF DEATH	MARCH 18, 1971
4 RACE WHITE	2 SEX F
5a WAS THE DECEDENT OF SPANISH ORIGIN?	5b IF YES SPECIFY MEXICAN, CUBAN, PUERTO RICAN ETC.
6 DATE OF BIRTH	Oct 30, 1915
7 AGE (in years last birthday)	55
IF UNDER 1 YEAR Months / Days	IF UNDER 24 HRS Hours / Minutes
8a PLACE OF DEATH — COUNTY HARRIS CO.	8b CITY OR TOWN (If outside city limits give precinct) HOUSTON, TEX
8c NAME OF (if not HOSPITAL OR INSTITUTION)	8d INSIDE CITY LIMITS? Yes
9 MARRIED NEVER MARRIED WIDOWED DIVORCED (Specify)	10 BIRTHPLACE (State or foreign country)
11 CITIZEN OF WHAT COUNTRY?	12 WAS DECEDENT EVER IN US ARMED FORCES? NO
13 SURVIVING SPOUSE (If wife give maiden name)	
14 SOCIAL SECURITY NO 3XX-XX-4706	15a USUAL OCCUPATION
15b KIND OF BUSINESS OR INDUSTRY	
16a RESIDENCE STATE	16b COUNTY HARRIS	16c CITY OR TOWN (If outside city limits give precinct)	16d STREET ADDRESS (If rural give location) 2224 DC	16e INSIDE CITY LIMITS?
17 FATHER'S NAME	18 MOTHER'S MAIDEN NAME

CAUSE OF DEATH

	IMMEDIATE CAUSE (Enter only one cause per line for (a), (b), (c))	Interval between onset and death
PART I	(a)	MARCH 8-18
	DUE TO OR AS A CONSEQUENCE OF	Interval between onset and death
	(b)	
	DUE TO OR AS A CONSEQUENCE OF	Interval between onset and death
	(c)	
PART II	OTHER SIGNIFICANT CONDITIONS — CONDITIONS CONTRIBUTING TO DEATH — BUT NOT RELATED TO CAUSE GIVEN IN PART I (a)	21 AUTOPSY? none

| 22a ACC SUICIDE HOM UNDET OR PENDING INVEST (Specify) N/A | 22b DATE OF INJURY (Mo. Day Yr) Mar 15, 71 | 22c HOUR OF INJURY 2 a.m. M | 22d DESCRIBE HOW INJURY OCCURRED |
| 22e INJURY AT WORK (Specify yes or no) | 22f PLACE OF INJURY — At home, farm street factory | 22g LOCATION STREET OR R F D NO | CITY OR TOWN | STATE |

23a To the best of my knowledge death occurred at the time, date and place and due to the cause(s) stated	24a On the basis of examination and/or investigation, in my opinion death occurred at the time, date and place and due to the cause(s) stated
CERTIFIER	
23b DATE SIGNED (Mo. Day Yr) MARCH 18, 1971	23c HOUR OF DEATH 4 a.m. M	24b DATE SIGNED (Mo. Day Yr) MARCH 18, 1971	24c HOUR OF DEATH M
23d NAME OF ATTENDING PHYSICIAN (Type or print)	24d PRONOUNCED DEAD (Mo. Day Year) On MARCH 18, 1971	24e PRONOUNCED DEAD (Hour) AT 4:20 M

25a BURIAL CREMATION REMOVAL (Specify)	25b DATE MARCH 18 1971	25c NAME OF CEMETERY OR CREMATORY unknown
25d LOCATION (City, town, or county)	(State)	26 SIGNATURE OF FUNERAL DIRECTOR OR PERSON ACTING AS SUCH
27a REGISTRAR'S FILE NO	27b DATE REC D BY LOCAL REGISTRAR	27c SIGNATURE OF LOCAL REGISTRAR

CHAPTER 8

Red Ribbons

"... I was taken up to heaven for a visit. Don't ask me whether my body was there or just my spirit, for I don't know; only God can answer that. But anyway, there I was in paradise, and heard things so astounding that they are beyond a man's power to describe or put in words ..." (II Corinthians 12:2-4, TLB).

For a moment I felt a strange sensation — like a fire whirring through my head. But there was no darkness, no pain searing through my bruised and battered body any longer. I could see everything that was happening — like I was above the room. Untouchable. Safe from the eerie trio watching my lifeless body.

And in the next instant, I was walking along what seemed like the apex of the universe. The light everywhere was the most unimaginable. There were no dark shadows. Everything shone with a glorious rose-tinted splendor.

Even though I seemed to be walking on billowing white ether, there was a firmness under my feet as I moved. Overhead was the most blue-hued sky I had ever seen. Every color, every sense was magnified innumerable times. A brilliantly lit magnetic force propelled me without any effort on my part.

Thoughts assaulted my mind, as if my brain had become a silent, drawing sponge. Even without a mirror, I realized that I was young again — beautiful, unwrinkled, with my hair raven-colored again and floating around me in the heavenly atmosphere. I felt twenty again — young, uninhibited, wearing a deep-purple robe. Human words cannot express the flood of emotions and sensations.

I could see the long train of the luxurious, purple robe flowing behind me. And looking down through the wisps of rosy mist, I could still see my earthly body lying on the steel cart, electrodes still fastened to my lifeless form, the guards watching as the nurse felt for a pulse. I saw her drop the stethoscope and look up with an evil grin which needed no words. Steel-and-Thunder ripped off the electrodes and yanked a sheet over my head with a brutal finality. I watched them wheel my dead body back to Room 120.

I knew, immediately, that they were going to tell the instigators what had happened, and they would begin to set the chain-of-events into motion to carefully dispose of my body.

But seeing all that didn't make me angry. I didn't hate Skinny or Steel-and-Thunder or the Follower anymore. I was completely at peace, far above pain and strife. My body was obviously dead, but I was more alive than ever.

Youth and love and contentment were fused together in an eternal, total sense of well-being. I knew, more than ever, the sense of that phrase I had heard in my childhood: "God's in His heaven — all's right with the world."

I had everything I had ever desired. A serenity suffused through every cell of my being. There were no worries, no questions. I seemed to know where I was going, and what I was going to do when I arrived there.

But the most unexplainable part was the peace, sweet peace. Like most people, I had always wondered how it would be to die. I had heard the preachers describe heaven back in Iowa at the country church where I accepted Jesus in my heart, but I always wondered, "Would I go in a hurry? Would I see angels?" There was always such a fear of the unknown before. But I felt such a distinctive harmony with everything that was happening to me. I don't know how long it took to pass from death to life. There was no longer any urgency of time. Peace overwhelmed time.

All at once, though light already surrounded me completely, a stunning glow appeared. Out of the white glow appeared the most beautiful Man I had ever seen. His shimmering robe was so dazzling it stunned my eyes. And around His waist was a belt that seemed to be formed of golden rope.

It was Jesus Christ! I had never given much thought to how He would look, except for pictures in books and portraits in art galleries. Still, I recognized Him immediately. I *knew* who He was. I thought of Peter, my son, as I looked at His beard and soft, brown, curly hair. He had the kindest, most compassionate face I had ever seen. And His eyes shone through me, as if He saw everything, knew everything. The most amazing thing was that it seemed so *right* for me to be with Him. I felt an inexpressible love flowing from Him to me, and from me to Him.

The peace and the love and the noticeable absence of darkness — *all* stood out in my mind.

At that moment, two regal-looking chairs materialized from nowhere. No one brought them. They were just *there*. They were like the antique high-back cherry chairs around our oversized dining room table in my childhood home.

Suddenly, I felt so comfortable, so *at home*. Jesus, in His wisdom, provided something with which I was already familiar. I had felt so much love in those chairs back in Iowa as we listened and talked to our parents. The love I felt then seemed to be magnified in those two chairs.

Jesus sat in one and I in the other. We were facing each other, so close we could have touched. We didn't actually touch then. We didn't need to. For some reason, some unexplainable fashion, I felt a part of Him. I was a *separate being,* yet at the same time an *extension of Him.*

All around us, as far as I could see, were the fleecy clouds and the azure skies. An ethereal rose sheen still colored everything around us. We were immersed in the milky clouds, and yet upon them. I was filled with supreme joy, a triumphant ecstasy far beyond anything humanly possible on earth. It was as if I had grasped the eternal truths at one time — like I was part of the same power as the Mighty One sitting with me. The complete freedom from care engulfed me totally.

The fear of death had fallen off like an old coat. It simply vanished. The Living Presence was giving out loving energy. I was speechless with awe, and I waited for Him to speak.

The entire heavenly sphere was like a vast garden, only I don't remember seeing flowers or golden buildings or anything like that. It was the effervescent, fragrant, presence of God which overwhelmed everything else. I couldn't take my eyes from His, and yet I knew everything around me. It was like many, many different levels of understanding and sensory perception flooding my mind.

We communicated for a time without words, effortlessly projecting our thoughts. Then He seemed to be looking over my head and smiling down at the earth below. Finally, He spoke audible words to me. Unforgettable words.

"Do you want to stay up here and work?" He asked. I can't describe His voice distinctly enough, but it was like gentle bells chiming in perfect, melodious harmony. He continued: "Or do you want to go back to earth? Today you are the judge, not the jury. Any time there is an interruption in the blueprint of your life that the Heavenly Father has given you, you have a choice."

For a moment (it's hard to say how long; there is no such thing as measured time), I weighed the pros and cons. I had known so much about everything as I was bathed by His Presence, but His question brought the unknown. I found it hard to think or answer.

Remaining there in God's garden was the most exciting and inviting existence I could ever want. There was such perfect peace, such goodness, such wisdom. Surely it would be better for me to stay in a place of eternal, pure love. I felt no pain there. I knew that to return to earth meant going back to that cruelly damaged body in the repulsive-smelling room where I was a prisoner with no way to escape.

Still, I felt drawn back there. There were unfinished projects on earth. My children were not yet grown and independent. They needed a mother's love. There were other endeavors I still had planned.

For some reason I remembered my parents. They had been such sticklers, insisting that each of the twelve of us always finished any project we started. When schoolwork or household chores were only half-done, Mother used to say, "You have the package wrapped, but you don't have the red ribbons on it yet."

How often I recalled her statement about the ribbons. And when a job was completed and well done, she never failed to compliment us — "That's a beautiful finishing touch. What lovely red ribbons. Now set it aside. You are ready for your next project."

It was good training that had stuck with me, even after I crossed over into that ethereal dimension.

"The blueprint of your life..." Jesus had said. Looking back, I could see how wisely He had put all the pieces together for me. Even before I had been conceived, I had been wonderfully designed. Accepting the Lord into my heart when I was five years old — that was hardly an accident. Even the prayer by the two Pentecostal women when I was a teenager — that was part of the plan. My successes, my struggles, my failures, my wealth — everything had been for a purpose.

Suddenly I felt a perfect assurance that whatever my choice would be, He could bring it to pass.

The matter of doing all things well had been so thoroughly ingrained into me. For some reason, as I looked back on my life, I knew there really was only one possible choice for me.

I looked at Him. He was giving out such loving energy. It was as if a great web of golden threads connected Him with me. It was like thousands of intravenous tubes filling my bloodstream with pure love.

I didn't want to leave Him, to leave His overpowering tenderness and kindness.

"My Lord," I spoke finally, still gratefully surprised that I knew Jesus *was* my Lord, "my work on earth is not done. I must wrap up many packages in red ribbons before my job is finished."

He knew, even before I spoke, what I was talking about. I didn't have to explain my decision. He understood.

Suddenly, I was on my way back.

CHAPTER 9

Return To Prison

In an instant, in accordance with the choice I had made, I was back on earth. In that split second, I was whisked from that familiar carved cherry chair to the bed in Room 120.

No longer in the flowing purple robe, I realized that I was lying, near-lifeless, in that once beautiful black blouse and slacks which had become caked with blood and body odors and with the sheet still covering my head.

I had left the splendor of that incredible light-filled dimension to come back to a stifling cubicle that reeked from the corner where I had relieved myself for ten days.

As I became conscious of where I was, streams of unusual sounding words flowed from my lips. I realized that the language was the same as that spoken by those women who had prayed with me in the "Holy Roller" church back in Iowa when I was a teenager. At first, I thought it was Hungarian.

I didn't understand the words, but from the feeling inside me, I knew that this unfamiliar tongue had something to do with the Holy Spirit and with praising God. It was the same feeling I had as I basked in the presence of Jesus.

But before I could ponder the meaning of the exotic words, I heard myself speaking in English again. The words, although familiar, were still strange. I had not decided of my own volition to say them. They simply came unbidden from my mouth: "God! Please help me! I cannot help myself."

I sensed that it was not I who was calling on God, but Someone inside me doing it for me — using my lips to form the words I needed to say.

The moment I uttered that prayer, I heard God answering me. His voice was like a living force, just like I had heard while I was sitting in the carved cherry chair. The words were powerful, mighty, loving, compelling, overwhelming. Each word was like an oasis of perfect love in the midst of a vast desert of fears.

"I am the Lord your God," He said. "I am here to help you, not to hurt you. Do not be afraid. Keep a spoon tonight when they bring your supper tray, and I will help you escape."

It seemed so unbelievable to me.

"Keep a spoon?" I thought crazily. "But they won't be bringing me a supper tray. They know I'm dead. And if I let them know I'm alive — God help me!"

I cringed at the thought of what they might do to me. And yet I knew that God had a blueprint for me, I wanted to be obedient. Somehow — someway I felt I could even face Steel-and-Thunder, the Follower, and Skinny again, if need be. I hoped that wouldn't happen.

Shoving my fears aside, I made myself speak — "Lord, whatever You say, whatever You want me to do, I'll say it. I'll do it."

Inwardly, I wondered, "But a spoon?" If I were going to escape somehow, I thought perhaps a knife would serve me better for prying off a lock, or for whatever He had in mind. I didn't vocalize my questions. Even back on earth, it hadn't taken me long to figure out who the Boss was.

"But I've been looking for a way out of here for ten whole days," I reminded Him. "If You can get me out, it will surely be a miracle."

His response startled me: "As My creation, you *are* a miracle!"

I didn't have time to accept that thought before He lovingly reassured me — "We *will* get you out of here."

I truly believed Him. The "blind faith" for which I had prayed several years before when I was in the church with my children — that "blind faith" was actually within my grasp!

Then another thought bombarded my mind. I remembered the letter I had received from the woman I didn't even know — "Everything is going to come out all right eventually," she had written. I could finally understand. I could believe.

I would have been content to lie there, just communing with my Lord. Something made me get up, however, and when I pushed myself up, I experienced the full impact of the pain. Weakness hung on my body like a heavy, agonizing, unseen force. My surroundings were as wretched as before. The uric and fecal stench, the dirty, bloodstained sheets — everything was just like it had been when I was dragged away to be electrocuted.

I looked at my "old friend and companion," the time-and-temperature sign across the street. I quickly calculated that I had been without any earthly consciousness for approximately six hours.

It was mid-afternoon, too early to request a tray. I remember that He had said, "Tonight."

As unbelievable as it all seemed, I knew that I had to obey, even when I could not comprehend.

I lay back quietly so I wouldn't attract my captors' attention. At first, my thoughts were nebulous and peaceful. I tried to remember the unearthly sphere I had visited. I wanted to remember His face — His words. I wished to bask again in the dimension so devoid of fear and concern. It seemed almost a sacrilege to move even a muscle.

But after awhile, I began trying to fit together all the pieces of the puzzle, even from months previous.

I could hardly bring myself to admit that my clinic manager was involved, but I forced myself to see that Zelda must have known what was going on. But how did she fit in the bigger picture?

Was Dr. Ronald Holmes the mastermind behind the psychological terror and diabolic shock treatments? He had that kind of reputation, especially when it meant a hefty payoff. He had been implicated before.

But what reason would either Zelda or Dr. Holmes have for trying to kill me?

I paid Zelda well, very generously. I had always treated her like a member of my own family.

I had never had any significant personal contact with Dr. Holmes, only brief phone conversations about some of his former patients who occasionally showed up at my Maritronics office. Most of those patients had experienced electroshock treatments, and were poor candidates for a healthy marriage until they could be brought back from such mental destruction.

And why, once I was "murdered," hadn't my body been disposed of?

I shook my head. Speculation about the baffling mystery was hopelessly futile. The last ten days had been the worst, most crushing part of the puzzle.

The thought flashed through my mind — what would happen if I asked my tormentors to let me see Dr.

Holmes? Would he come? Would he reveal anything to me? No. At least for that evening, I didn't want to do anything that might jeopardize whatever God had planned.

And even that was confusing. If God had the power to take me away, then allow me to return, why couldn't He just whisk me away to safety? A spoon? After being with Him, after sitting across from Him — a spoon seemed almost like a joke. But I knew I had to trust Him. I had no other choice.

I decided to spend the waiting time to record my out-of-this-world experiences. Reaching under the mattress I felt for my pen and the little scraps of paper. They were still there.

"Praise God!"

Could it have been only the day before that I had been jotting down the most recent, unspeakable horrors?

When it was nearly dark, I knew what I had to do. Knowing the danger, I forced myself toward the door. My heart was pounding inside my stiff, sore chest.

Bracing myself, I began pounding on the door. I felt sure the guards would still be outside, no longer to prevent my escape, but to make sure that the wrong people didn't discover my body before everything was in order.

To my surprise, it wasn't Steel-and-Thunder who opened to my knocking. It was the Follower. By comparison to the globby giant, he seemed almost meek.

Nothing can describe the look on his face when he opened the door. It was as if a ghost had knocked for him!

"Can I have my supper tray?" I asked.

I only saw his ashen face for a split second. Without a word, he slammed the door. I could hear his retreating footsteps out in the hall.

Breathless moments later, I heard approaching footsteps. Steel-and-Thunder burst into my room. His hate-filled eyes swept the room, making a swift, brooding analysis. Then, like a hulking coward, he whirled, wild-eyed, slammed the door behind him, and pounded out of earshot. I could only imagine he had rushed away to inform some higher authority that I was alive — maybe Skinny, or Dr. Holmes, or Zelda (it was still so unthinkable).

I had asked for my supper just as the door slammed. I hoped that the Follower heard. Thankfully, before long, Jane, the petite nurse's aide, appeared.

The food on the tray was like many times before — the carefully perforated carton of milk, some awful substance which looked like stew warmed over several times. At least the hard roll looked harmless.

With Steel-and-Thunder temporarily out of the way, I was able to persuade Jane to bring me a glass of water from the fountain I had seen in the hall. She did. Then the door closed behind her. I was alone.

I gnawed gingerly on the hard roll, trying to avoid the teeth which seemed loosest. The water I drank was heavenly, even with my cracked lips and parched throat. The cool liquid tasted like life being poured back into me. I thanked God for it.

I slopped the morbid-looking stew around on the tray, pretending to eat some of it for the Follower who watched me through the small window in the door. Then, as I continued my act, I turned my back to the door and slipped the spoon down into one of the two skinny pockets on the sleeveless black coat of my pantsuit. Even during that tense moment, I was smitten with how perfectly designed that pocket seemed to be for the spoon.

God saw to the rest of the details as the strange sequence continued to unfold. At six o'clock, both guards returned for my tray. Always before, they had hovered over me when it was time to take the tray away, and every piece of silver, every dish had been painstakenly accounted for. They had always checked under the pillow and sheets, even feeling all over my body as if I were a criminal.

Incredibly, this time there was none of that. Maybe they were afraid to be around me. They kept looking at me in total unbelief. It was spooky. Eerie.

Whatever the reason, it was the only time in ten days they failed to search me before they left the room.

CHAPTER 10

The Spoon

At nine o'clock, God began to instruct me in His plan for my escape. It was totally absurd for me; all my life, I had based every decision on logic.

He knew exactly what I was thinking. In fact, His first words were, "As soon as you learn that I am not confined to logic . . ."

As He paused, I felt ashamed of my "rational" thought about saving a knife instead of the spoon from the dinner tray. I silently acknowledged Him. I felt immediate, gentle forgiveness flowing through me. Then the Voice continued:

"As soon as you learn that I am not confined to logic, that I am supernatural and super-normal, we can work together."

I wanted to ponder those words, but God said, "Let me show you who We are." He hadn't appeared to me in bodily form as Jesus had while I was in that unearthly sphere. However, I instantly saw a ball of light which totally filled and illuminated the dingy room.

"We are One — Father, Son, and Holy Ghost," the Voice announced. Then the bright orb split into three separate balls which formed a triangle. "Now we are separate."

I *knew*, like I had experienced total knowledge while in that other dimension, that God the Father was the shining spherical light at the top of the triangle; Jesus was the one below on His right; and the Holy Spirit on His left. Though They spoke as one, each member of the Trinity was identifiable by His distinctive voice. The Father had a deep, booming voice with resonant overtones like I had never heard before. Jesus' voice was tender and compassionate, just like when we sat in the chairs. The Holy Spirit sounded somewhat like the nicest teacher I ever had — who had taught me law and psychology.

"Now We are One again."

As God spoke, the three lights merged into a single brilliant mass. The radiance took full possession of the entire room. It was light, but it was also pure love, and it seemed to assume the shape of the space it filled. For a brief moment, I felt an arm enveloping and holding mo.

Then, just as if a switch had clicked, the light suddenly left the room. The Voices remained, teaching me about God and carefully laying the groundwork for my escape.

It all still seemed so absurd to me, even after all I had experienced during that incredible day. I had so little knowledge of God, of His Word, of His ways. I kept wondering why I had been singled out for all that was happening to me. It was just too much for me to take in.

As though my uneasiness and lack of knowledge were understood, the Voices instructed me — separately and together, but always in total agreement and harmony with one another. I could always identify the Person who was speaking, just from the unmistakable sound of His voice.

It was the Holy Spirit — the Teacher — who gave the first command. "Tell the guards you have had a rough day and are going to bed early."

I laughed outloud. It was like a joke — the understatement of the century. For some reason, God didn't seem to mind that I laughed. I felt like a child, open and innocent and wide-eyed before Him.

Though I wasn't in the habit of telling the guards anything, I rose from my bed and knocked on the door to deliver the message. The Follower responded almost immediately, peering cautiously as he opened the door ajar.

"I'm going to bed early, so please don't bother me," I announced, startled at the authority rising in my voice. "I'm very tired."

He seemed caught so completely off-guard that I decided to blurt out another question: "Is it possible for me to see Dr. Holmes before I retire?"

"No," the Follower stammered, "h-h-he left early this afternoon. But I'll tell him . . . you want to see him — to see him in the mornin'."

He shut the door softly, clicking the dead bolt back in place. I'd never seen a more confused man. I almost felt sorry for him. Almost.

As soon as the door was closed, the Lord gave me my next instruction: "Now remove your wig head from its bedside stand, and write on the Styrofoam as I tell you."

Each new step seemed more puzzling to me than the last. And I kept wondering if the Follower outside the door was hearing God's voice like I was. I'm sure he hadn't, since he stayed outside the room, but I couldn't understand why.

So I took the black wig off the stand, and I wrote a

message that God dictated:

> Dear Dr. Holmes —
> You may do anything you wish with this head — but leave mine intact.
>
> — Dr. Wagner

It was as if I was sharing some kind of inside joke with God. I had never thought of Him like that before. He had always been some faraway relic, like many of the religious artifacts I had seen. I was *enjoying* just being in His presence.

Next, God had me place the curly, black wig back on the Styrofoam stand and put it on the bed. Then He showed me exactly how to adjust the pillows below it to resemble my body. In the outlined darkness, it really did look like a person in the bed.

"Now, pull the spread up."

I smiled at the little details. Since that first hideous day, I had always slept with the blood-stained spread over my head, like a small child hoping that the thin material would keep away my very real boogeymen.

"Now, hide behind the curtain," He continued. "At exactly 9:20, the guards will shine a light through the window in the door and think you are fast asleep. They will not make another check tonight."

I knew I had to follow every instruction carefully. My life depended upon every word He spoke.

The drapes, like the bedspread, were made from drab material designed more for durability than beauty. Still, the drapes were fully lined. I was grateful for the added body and bulk as I hid behind the folds and flattened myself firmly against the window. My nostrils twitched as I stood. I was almost amused at myself, even in the midst of my unfolding life-and-death drama; I stood there wishing I could toss those dusty, foul-smelling drapes into a washing machine until they were fresh and clean again.

I made sure that I was completely concealed from

the soon-coming gaze of the guards. Even my chic black boots, once shiny, but then caked and stained, were not visible. The years of use had made the drapes sag, even overlapping down on the floor several inches.

Once sure that I was as safe as possible, I could do nothing but wait, trying to keep my tense breathing from moving the drapes. I watched the blinking time-and-temperature sign. I hoped it would be the last time I would have to spend the night with my old, continually flashing "friend."

As I waited, the Holy Spirit spoke: "Say this after Me — 'Lord, I'm one of Your little lost sheep. I've lost my way. Please take me back into the fold.' "

What? I thought, "But that's something just like a child would say!" So strange. Nevertheless, I repeated the words.

And as I spoke, a rush of power came upon me, so powerful and great. I didn't understand, but I knew there must be some urgent purpose for that surging power.

Then I saw the flickering flashlight beam shining briefly through the small window of the locked door. I strained to see the flashing sign across the street. It was 9:20 p.m. Exactly. Just as God had said it would be!

Within a split second after the lightbeam disappeared from the room, Jesus spoke clearly to me:

"Now, let us get to work!"

CHAPTER 11

Freedom

Even before Jesus finished His command, something inside me exploded. I knew instinctively that it meant I was to take down the Plexiglas wall.

"So *that* is what the spoon is for!" I breathed.

It seemed so impossible to even think about, but the supernatural assurance in that beautiful Voice, and the Holy Spirit's powerful surge when I repeated those words both made me confident that I could do *anything* He asked.

When I stepped from behind the drapes and looked at the two hundred Phillips-head screws (I knew full well how many there were; I had counted them so many times trying to keep contact with reality) which held the huge sheet of Plexiglas in place, I faltered. It seemed almost like a comedy of errors for me to be tackling such a formidable task with only a spoon as my "tool."

Absurd or not, I had no other alternative but to listen and follow.

"Just show me the way, Lord," I prayed. It was more sincere, more urgent than any phrase I had previously spoken. "I'll do *anything* You say." I was willing, but I also knew the strength would have to come from Him.

As soon as I said the last words, Jesus verbalized the answer to my asked and unasked questions: "I am the way, the truth, and the life: no man comes to the Father but by Me." It sounded like something I had heard in the Bible from my childhood days. My courage soared!

God immediately showed me how to use the tool He had provided. I took the spoon from my pocket and hesitatingly inched it up to one of the screws. The bowl of the spoon proved to be a surprisingly adequate screwdriver. After I stretched to remove a screw from the top left of the Plexiglas panel, He directed me to a corresponding screw on the lower right. I didn't even understand the impact of what I was doing at the time, but everything was being done in perfect order so that the weight of the plastic sheet was always evenly distributed. My battered, scabbed fingers had become endowed with a super-human strength. I knew it had come from God. There was no need for questions any longer.

Though it had probably not been a long time since the barrier had been installed (judging from the construction materials I had noticed that first, fateful day when I entered the hospital), many of the screws were already rusted in place, probably from the rain which seeped in around the outer windows.

Removing those screws would have been impossible under normal circumstances (I could hardly get the non-rusted side and top screws loose), but when I came to the lower, rusted screws, as soon as the spoon neared each one, a wave of supernatural energy would course through my arm. I even had to steady my shaking right hand with my left at each surge. And each time, the rust would dissolve right before my eyes.

Even for someone who had gone through an incredible day like mine had been, there was something almost too unbelievable about instantly dissolving rust. But it happened not just once, but repeatedly — each time I reached another of the rusted, lower screws.

Truthfully, I hardly remembered that a guard was undoubtedly outside my door. For some reason, I was able to work without fear, knowing that God must have done something unusual already to keep the guards occupied from their usual sporadic, flashlight searching forays into my room.

So for hours I worked on the heavy layer of Plexiglas, leaning my shoulder against it, supporting it with my left knee so it wouldn't fall.

To help me reach the top screws easier, I pushed the nightstand over against the window. One by one, from one side to the other, I kept removing the pieces of spiraled metal. Each one meant that I was that much closer to freedom!

I noticed from the sign that it was nearly one o'clock. I had almost finished removing all the screws. So much had happened.

Still, I was hardly prepared for God's baffling instruction. It had absolutely nothing to do with removing the window.

"I want you to pray for David," He said. "At this moment, the engines of his plane are stopping in the middle of the sky."

"David?" I thought, completely confused. "Who is David?" I wondered what some unknown man named David had to do with me, especially at the very time when I was trying to escape. "Why do You want me to pray for him?"

God's quick answer assaulted my senses, shocking me beyond belief — "David is the man who plotted your kidnapping, but he will never hurt you again. Where he is going, there you will never be."

"Plotted my kidnapping!" My mind raced. "Someone I don't even know? But why? Money? Did that man named David need money?" I had thought of robbery as the motive before, but it seemed unlikely. My jewelry and purse had been taken from me that first day. Robbery certainly couldn't have made someone put me through such a living hell.

I was both dumbfounded and bewildered at the incredulous situation. How could I pray for someone who had ordered me killed?

"I don't even know how to pray for myself," I argued. "How can I pray for somebody else?"

"I will teach you," He said patiently. When He spoke, it sounded familiar, like words from the Bible. I was told to repeat those words — "Father, forgive him. He knew not what he was doing."

Finished with that prayer, I was still puzzled. "Lord," I asked, "why did You have me pray for that man if he's going to hell anyway?" It seemed like such a useless waste of time. I still had much to do before I could escape.

But God wouldn't let the issue drop. "When you discover all he has done," the Voice spoke, "you will be angry. This forgiveness is necessary to keep anger and bitterness, to keep resentment and rebellion from lodging in your heart and becoming a part of you. That would be a definite hindrance to your life with me."

"When you discover all he has done?" I wondered if God meant there was more than what I had endured already. Suddenly I thought of my children. Oh, I hoped they were all right. Then I wondered about my house and my businesses.

But I had no time to dwell on the "all he has done" possibilities racing through my mind. Even in the midst of the worst imaginable hell, I wanted to be optimistic. I refused to believe that anything bad had happened to

Peter or Kimberli.

"I'm alive!" I urged myself on silently. "God is with me. Soon I will be breathing fresh, free air again. Soon this will all be over."

It took me three and a half hours, but the last screw was finally out.

And as I pressed against the heavy sheet of plastic to keep it from crashing to the floor, God clearly directed me to place two fingers of my right hand under the bottom edge of the Plexiglas to balance it. Then I was told to use my left hand to steady it, and to lay it down onto the floor.

"Two fingers?" I already realized how heavy the large barrier was, but my mind had already stopped trying to protest God's directions — each had worked out perfectly.

Using my foot, I pushed the bed over to make more room on the floor, then I simply did as I had been told. As I put two fingers under the edge, the heavy panel became almost weightless. I was able to lift it effortlessly. Noiselessly I laid my first major obstacle onto the floor.

Next came the outer windows. Looking down below, I could see the faint outlines of prickly-type bushes beneath all three of the windows, but the lowest bush was beneath the window nearest the street. I quickly chose that one as the best.

I began to attack the second army of reluctant screws with my increasingly worn spoon.

I wanted to go on, but my hands were completely worn out. Progress seemed hopelessly slow. I knew God was helping me, but I didn't know — at that moment — if I could take any more. I looked around at the horrible room.

"God," I cried, "I can't do anything else. I only want this nightmare to be over. Finished."

But it had been *my* choice to return, my determination

to return to my battered, weak, swollen body. As my strength ebbed dangerously low, I began to wonder if I had been wise in that decision — red ribbons, or not.

"If you do not keep going," God urged, "you cannot survive. Tomorrow will be too late. You *have* to keep going."

Once more I found myself exercising that "blind faith" for which I had earlier prayed. It was totally impossible to continue in my own strength. But I had to move first in obedience. He was willing to help, to be that strength, but only if I gave Him my resolute weakness.

As I reached to begin unscrewing the pieces of metal holding the outer window, another startling surge of power jolted through my right arm, through me. Almost effortlessly, like a powerful magnet, the spoon drew the screw from the edges of the glass.

The sign pulsated, "2 a.m." I was almost finished with the window. Then, like before, the Holy Spirit interrupted my labors with another eerie request.

"I want you to pray for George," He stated.

"George? George who?" I wondered if it was the George who had worked with me on my last medical research project. I knew when I hired him that he had gone through an alcohol problem in the past, but he had assured me that it was conquered. I had found him more than competent as a worker. "That George?"

"Yes, *that* George!" the Holy Spirit affirmed. "At this very moment, his car is on Highway 10, just a few miles from here, traveling ninety miles an hour and crashing into the back of a flatbed truck!"

"Oh, no!" I gasped. But I didn't argue. Earnestly I prayed the same prayer for George which God had given me for David: "Father, forgive him. He knew not what he was doing."

When I prayed those words of forgiveness, I became almost drunk with the supernatural flow of energy and joy. Light as a feather! It seemed that once more I had escaped my tormented body — not in death like before, but into eternal life, right on the spot!

Still, I couldn't help questioning why the people involved in my kidnapping were dying.

"God, how can you be a God of love and let those men die?"

He didn't defend Himself, but said clearly, "Vengeance is mine, saith the Lord. Touch not Mine anointed. You are My anointed child. You were anointed by Me before you were put into your mother's womb."

"Anointed? Me?" I wondered what He meant, but there was no explanation given. I sensed that I would understand someday.

When there were only a few screws left to remove, the Holy Spirit spoke to me again: "You have been taken through the fire, and you are an obedient child. Now, what do you want?"

I was startled by such an abrupt, unexpected statement. It seemed too much like a fairytale. I was never one to accept anything from anyone. It started back when, as a teenager, I shunned the silver spoon for charting my own course. Prior to my imprisonment, I never felt I needed anything much from anyone. I thought it was just my independent spirit, but I had been shown that it was arrogance and egotism. Still, I didn't like accepting "charity" from anyone, not even God.

"I need more time," I breathed.

"You have an eternity."

I just couldn't figure out what He was talking about. I continued working on the final screws, but my mind sifted through something I wanted from God.

"I could ask to be delivered without having to jump through the window," I thought, "or I could request to be spared future death."

Just as when we sat in the chairs, Jesus responded

to my unspoken flow of ideas. Immediately He said, "I am the resurrection and the life: he that believeth in me, though he were dead, yet shall he live: and whosoever liveth and believeth in me shall never die."

I realized I hardly needed to make a request about jumping. Someone who could take me beyond and back could certainly get me safely to the ground from a third-story window in a Houston hospital.

Still working with the spoon, I asked another mental question — "You know, Lord, so many people are miserable. I would like to make people happy and well."

"What do you think you've been doing all your life?" He asked. "I gave you that gift, like my anointing, long before you were in your mother's womb."

Looking back, a realization broke through. Of the businesses I had started, people had been made happier and healthier. I *had* a ministry, even when I hardly knew the Lord. I hadn't even been aware of it. Certainly I had never thought of my work in that light.

"Name something for yourself," the Holy Spirit instructed.

That hardly seemed difficult. The most important concern in my personal life was my children. Kimberli, eighteen, was a senior at Incarnate Word, a finishing school in San Antonio. Peter, two years older than his sister, was a freshman at the University of St. Thomas in Houston. Their education was far from finished, so I asked God to give my children knowledge and the wisdom to be productive.

"Your children will be educated in My name," He affirmed, "but that's for them. What about something for yourself?"

I still felt too proud to be comfortable taking something from Him for myself. My pride was crumbling, however, and there was something very dear to me. In spite of my work with Maritronics which had helped

150,000 couples become happily wed, I was another of Houston's divorce statistics.

"How about a happy marriage for me?"

"In my time," He promised, "not in yours."

Still perplexed, I noticed that the work had been progressing rapidly while the unusual conversation took place.

When all the screws were out of the glass panel covering the window, I laid the glass out on the floor as quietly as possible.

Only the bars remained — heavy, black, iron rods caked with weathered rust. Upon quick investigation, I found that they fitted snugly into the top of the lower sash which extended to the top of the window casing. That was so the extreme outer window could not be raised.

"How can I ever remove these bars?" I wondered.

I knew I had to work fast. My captors were just a few feet away, outside the door. God had said that they would not check on me again, but I knew the noises of knocking the bars loose could signal my escape attempt.

But as soon as I asked about removing the bars, God showed me precisely how to force the tip of the spoon into the minute space at the base of each bar, to press down slightly on the handle, and to pop the bar loose from its niche in the top of the lower sash.

I did exactly as He said. Amazingly, each popped right out! A knife could never have provided the necessary leverage but would have bent or slipped out. Oh, God's wisdom!

Once more, I was interrupted by the Holy Spirit to pray for a man named Don.

"Don?" I knew immediately who he was — a semi-retired NASA aerospace engineer. He had earlier joined Maritronics. He had been very talkative, warm, and friendly. He had even told me that he wanted to

become a minister, and I had introduced him to someone who helped him obtain the necessary credentials.

The prayer I was told to say was much different for
Don than for George and David. I repeated after Him,
"Open the doorway of Heaven wide, Lord. Don is coming
in."

"But why was Don entering Heaven now? What had
happened to him? We had become good friends, or so
I thought. "Was he involved in my kidnapping, too?" My
unspoken questions were left unanswered.

I felt an uncommon urgency to forge ahead. It was
almost three o'clock. I pushed up the window sash,
and an incredibly fresh, fragrant gulf breeze caressed
my senses. It was so different from the foul atmosphere in which I had been trapped for ten days.

As I looked out the third-story window, the ground
below seemed much farther away than I imagined.
There, just thirty feet down, an impossible leap away,
lay my freedom! With it so close, and yet so far, the
poignancy of the moment overwhelmed me. Out there,
down there were clothes and stores and soft drinks
and hot baths. Life! It all seemed like such a dream.

I was still in Room 120 with the beatings, urine
stench, injections, and death. But I was on the edge of
life.

"What do I do now?" I asked.

"Petti Wagner, walk out in faith as you have done all
your life. Jump, and I will catch you! If you take the first
step, I will take you by the hand every inch of the way. I
did not make the water firm for Peter until he took the
first step, nor did I save Isaac until Abraham lifted up
the knife."

I knew it was impossible to jump to the ground and
not be hurt, but I couldn't afford to start doubting Him
then. In the previous hours, God had demonstrated
His willingness to lead. All I had to do was obey. The
rusted screws, the spoon, the instructions — *every-*

thing had been precise.

That "blind faith" became a matter of life and death. The captors were still there ... somewhere. I *had* to jump.

I took one last look around, then remembered the little scraps of paper on which I had chronicled my ordeal. I grabbed them from under the mattress and stuffed them into my left jacket pocket. With my right hand, I dumped the lithium tablets into another pocket. There were more than a hundred, and I wanted them as evidence when I escaped. I also kept my precious spoon with me.

I was ready.

At the window, the breezes swept over me again, drawing me. I stepped over the low sill. For a moment, I perched precariously on the window ledge.

The supreme test of trust had arrived — that moment when I lived or died. I *could* fall into a crumpled heap on the ground. Or ...? Only God could help me. There were no other alternatives.

Poised, I lifted my hands. No more waiting. Then I leaped into the murky darkness.

CHAPTER 12

Land Of The Living

That was three in the morning. Friday, March 19, 1971.

I jumped toward the bush, but my body seemed almost weightless. I landed completely unhurt. Suddenly I was running for my life along Westheimer Road, my boots scraping as each stride touched the pavement. The street was strangely deserted. I was gasping for each torturous breath, moving faster than I thought possible. Every step put more distance between me and that nightmarish hell.

Westheimer was being widened. The roadway was in a bad state of repair — muddy from recent rains, full of potholes. Thankfully, there was enough light from street lamps to avoid the potholes as I forced myself onward. So weak from the torture and escape, I knew that only sheer terror and God's help kept pushing me. On and on. Like a bad dream. Running, yet as if in slow motion.

Far down the road behind me, I saw headlights. The

warning of the Holy Spirit was immediate and unmistakable: "HIDE IN THE DITCH!"

Although I didn't want to stop anywhere until I had
reached a place of safety, I forced myself to obey.

All my life I had been totally afraid of darkness, but I
made myself scramble down a grassy bank into the
ditch which had been dredged alongside the road (as
part of the construction/repair process). Torn between
the hysterical desire to scream and the knowledge
that God was guiding me, I lay flat, trembling, every
breath searing my parched throat. I could see the faint
outline of weeds, broken bottles, beer cans, and other
trash covered with muddy water. I hoped there were
no snakes or rodents.

After a seeming eternity, the car sped by. They hadn't
seen me!

Climbing back up to the pavement, I forced my feet
to run again. The night was dark and overcast. As I
raced along the half-finished road, I could see that one
side was an open field. On the other side were buildings. Perhaps some of them contained people, but
that was doubtful. It was after three in the morning.
The only thing I knew to do was to keep running.

My right foot struck a rock. I wanted to stop and rest.
My painful gasps throbbed through my body as I also
felt the sting of salty sweat on my battered cheeks. My
hands were bleeding from scrambling down the ditch.
Wounds reopened. Had I come that far to pass out on
the deserted street?

"No!" I kept forcing myself on, my eyes searching
frantically in the murkiness to see if anyone was following me. I felt as if I had been stumbling along for an
eternity, though I had probably only run less than a
half-mile. I just wanted someone to rescue me before I
collapsed from exhaustion. Too much had already
happened to me.

"Headlights!" A second vehicle was coming from the

direction of the hospital. Friend or ...? Maybe help? But before headlights beamed upon me, I received the same apprehensive warning as before.

Again I concealed myself in the darkness until the car was out of sight. At that hour in the morning, traffic was naturally sparse. Although I appreciated my Father's protection, I wondered if it really was necessary for Him to be quite so selective.

"I'm sorry, Lord. I trust you."

I started to run again, and as a third vehicle approached I expected to be cautioned by the Holy Spirit as twice before. This time, however, His voice was relaxed, encouraging. There was little urgency.

"This is a child of the Father," I heard quite audibly. "He will take you where you want to go." It was the Teacher's voice, as if He were saying, "See, Petti? I have everything under control!"

I stopped running and stood beside the street, panting. A late-model white Chevrolet sedan slowed to a stop. There were no other cars in sight. I wondered if it were a trap — if my hell was going to start all over. Yet, I had heard the reassuring words. I was almost too tired to care anymore. Was my nightmare finally ending? I choked on a combination of relief and terror.

The front door on the passenger side of the car swung open. The inside lights went on automatically, illuminating the driver, a pleasant-faced young man. He called out to me, "I'm a newspaper distributor for the *Chronicle*."

Was it finally over? I held back the sobs.

He continued — "You are a child of God! Get in. I'm to take you where you want to go!"

My mind wasn't prepared for that startling statement. Though I had experienced so much with God during the past hours, that was my first contact with another person who heard like that from the Holy Spirit.

It was so new. Was I crazy? Worse, was I dead? My. Father's inner voice responded instantly to my racing thoughts: "You are very much alive, and your sanity is insured by Me." It was too much!

I stared at the driver. He had reached out to help me in. I took his hand and slid into the front seat, cringing in regret as my filthy clothes touched his clean up-holstery.

For some reason, I couldn't help questioning him, "Why did you say *that* to me?"

He was already moving again. He chuckled softly — "I could see you a long ways away. Why, just look at you. You have light all around you. You're lighting up the whole inside of my car!"

My mouth fell open. Indeed — although the door was closed and the overhead light off — the interior of the car was as bright as day!

Though it seemed so strange and mysterious, some-how the glory of God had enveloped me. I had never heard of anything like that. My mind raced to under-stand.

"Were you in an accident?" the man said as the car continued motoring.

My appearance certainly needed an explanation, but I didn't want to arouse his curiosity. I especially didn't want to return to the scene.

"Yes," I breathed, "an accident. Please take me to University Park. My aunt lives there. I'll call the police from there." Everything was still so unanswered. I didn't know who was involved. I didn't dare go near my home or office alone. I didn't know what — or whom — I might find there.

The *Chronicle* distributor had to make several stops to deliver his papers, so it was almost 4 a.m., according to the car's dashboard clock, when we arrived at Aunt Anna's house. The young man waited to make sure I was okay while I rang the doorbell.

Suddenly, the full impact of my appearance hit me.

"What will Aunt Anna think?" I wondered. My battered face, the left eye horribly damaged, my dark locks now white, all the dried blood on my filthy, rancid clothes — I hardly looked like the old me.

I needn't have concerned myself about those gruesome details which ordinarily would have alarmed her.

When my aunt came to the door, her mouth fell open. Temporarily speechless, she unfastened the screen door and pulled me inside. I thought she was still shocked at the damage.

When she finally spoke, Aunt Anna exclaimed, "Petti Wagner! Where on earth have you been? Somebody has painted you with phosphorus from the top of your head to the tip of your toes!"

She saw it too — the glow which signaled my rescuer! I knew I had been in the presence of God all those hours, but I didn't understand what was going on. I fled to the nearest mirror to see for myself.

Even after what the young man and my aunt had said, I was hardly prepared for the reflection peering back at me. My face, disfigured and bruised, had a radiance like a golden-white sheen. The white hair only added to the unearthly glint. Even with my putrid clothing, I had an aura surrounding me. Momentarily, as I totally ignored my thoroughly bewildered aunt, I simply stood in childlike wonder. I had never heard of such a thing. Even with everything I had seen, all that — the carved cherry chairs, the purple robe, His eyes — had been in a world so far away. Even the orbs of light, the spoken instructions, the melting rust — all of that had been in my hellish prison. But the neon-like radiation, that was visible evidence my rescuer *and* my aunt had seen, too. The supernatural had continued, even in the land of the living!

I was jolted back to the moment when I remembered my awestruck aunt. I told her very briefly what I had been through. I could see that she believed me. That was very important at that point. I hardly believed it all myself! Relief flooded through my jagged emotions. I could hardly contain the alternate sobs and joyful cries. How glad I was to see my aunt. How happy I was that she had not experienced a heart attack, as I had been told over the telephone before the grinding ordeal began.

"Jesus," I thought, as we talked, and as the hot bath water ran for the most necessary scrubbing of my life, "how absolutely wonderful to be free!"

I felt such exhilaration, yet such uncertainty. There was so much to be done, so many unanswered questions.

As the water continued flowing into the tub, I went to the telephone. With an air of finality, I touched the numbers on the telephone, then listened intently as the phone rang.

I knew, even before the desk sergeant answered the telephone, that the next hours and days would answer many shattering questions. I just hoped that my once-comfortable life could someday return to normal. How little I knew!

Olive (Petti) Peet — age 14

Olive Peet Wagner (1953)

Christmas 1953 — just before Kimberli was born

Karl and Petti Wagner at press conference for Petti's Herbagere Company — September, 1955

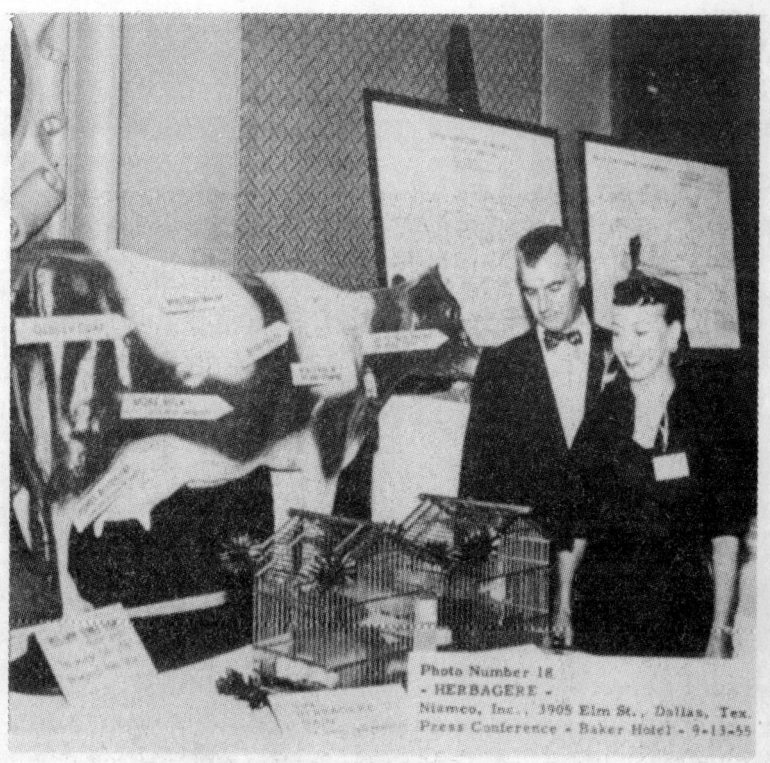

Photo Number 18
- HERBAGERE -
Niamco, Inc., 3905 Elm St., Dallas, Tex.
Press Conference - Baker Hotel - 9-13-55

Karl and Petti Wagner

Karl and Petti Wagner

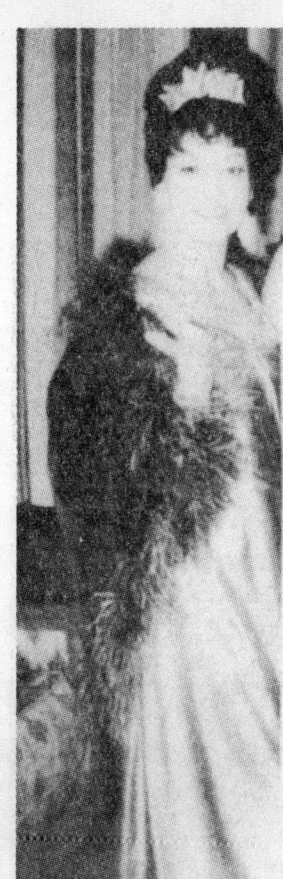

Petti Wagner

**Petti Wagner
White House January 1971**

**With Vice President
Bush 1971**

**With Texas
Congressman Collins
1971**

**"SOUTHWEST HOSPITAL" EAST WING —
arrow marks "Room 120"**

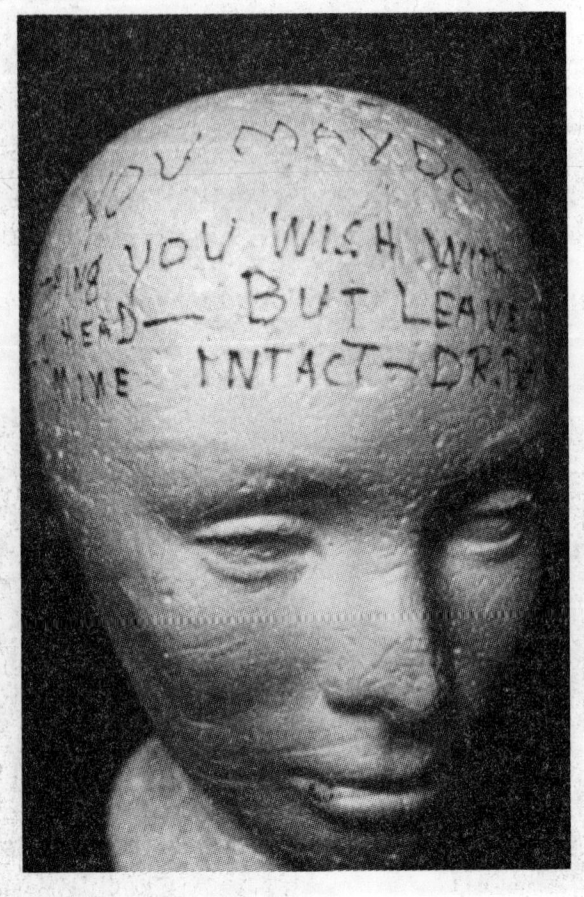

The original, inscribed Styrofoam wig stand

**Petti and Peter with Congressman Allen Steelman
1973**

Dr. Petti Wagner

Kimberli — writer, actress, singer, and composer

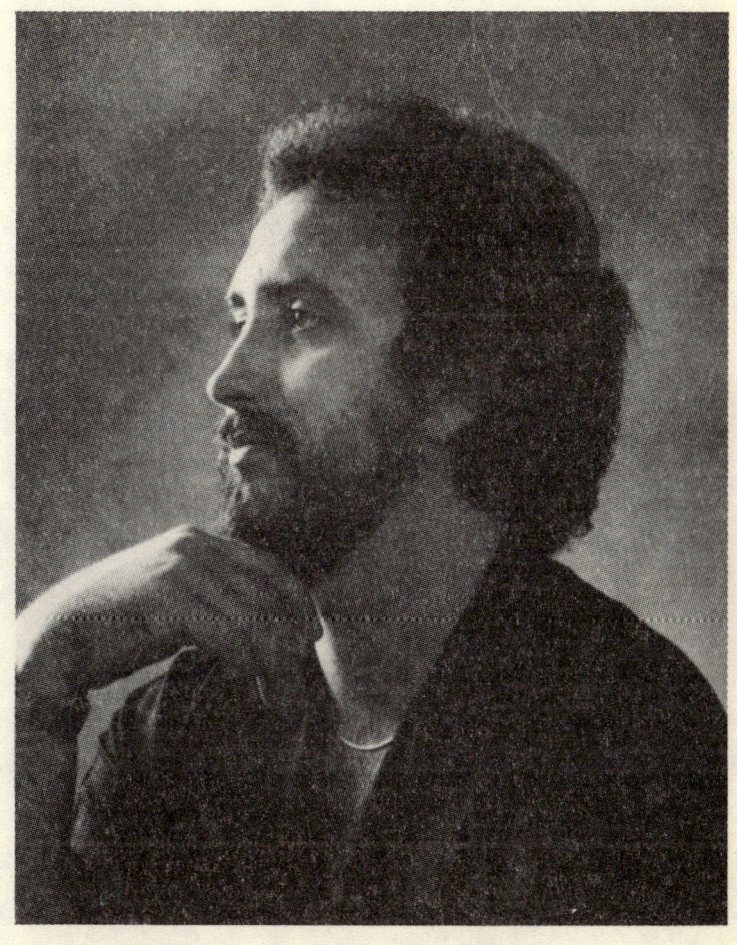

MY SON — Peter David Wagner III
Named after two very famous men

**The only picture remaining on my wall
was this one of Jesus.**

Picture taken after the kidnapping

Dr. Wagner with Pat Robertson on the 700 Club

CHAPTER 13

Tangled Web

And I will bring the blind by a way that they know not; I will lead them in paths that they have not known: I will make darkness light before them, and crooked things straight. These things will I do unto them, and not forsake them, (Isaiah 42:16).

"Houston Police Department . . ."

I tried to sound calm: "Something horrible has happened to me! I need a bodyguard at all times until I can discover who is behind what happened — until I can find out why." The sergeant put me through to Officer Al Johnson — "I'll come immediately, Dr. Wagner. Stay right there."

Aunt Anna threw my filthy clothes into her washing machine while I slipped into the soothing bath water. I knew I would need the clothes, and Aunt Anna was tiny; I couldn't have worn hers if I tried.

As the clothes were tumbling in the dryer, she brought me a wraparound robe. She wanted me to sleep right then, but I was too keyed up.

We talked quickly. Officer Johnson hadn't arrived yet.

For ten days I had wondered why no one had come for me. Even if Zelda and some of my employees were working against me, there were many other people who should have been concerned — my children, Doctors Le Roy and John McGuire (both friends as well as colleagues), Luci (my faithful maid), even Aunt Anna. I had felt so betrayed, so alone. I had been as deeply hurt by their unexplainable, uncharacteristic lack of concern about me.

Anna answered that painful question quickly — "Zelda called me the night you left. She said that you had decided to vacation in Acapulco for awhile. She also said something very puzzling — that I should report to her any strange telephone calls concerning your whereabouts."

So that was it! I had gone to Acapulco many times before. It was a special refuge to me where I could soak in the sun, rest peacefully without the constant jangling of a telephone, and enjoy the sumptuous meals and nightlife. It was the perfect explanation for Zelda to use when I had suddenly disappeared. No wonder no one seemed concerned about me (although I later found out that many were).

Back in familiar surroundings, the events of the past ten days seemed even more hideous. It was like I was suddenly pinching myself and waking up from a nightmare. I knew I had to keep holding on to God's promise — "You are very much alive, and I have insured your sanity." It had happened!

But if the nightmare of terror was real, then my life was still in danger. Undoubtedly the guards were already scurrying around trying to find me. It was early morning. Surely they had checked and found me missing from Room 120.

Officer Al Johnson arrived. With him there, Aunt Anna

talked me into sleeping awhile before tackling the monumental task of unraveling the tangled web. She didn't have to coerce me. I was so weak, so very tired. I longed to sleep between the delightfully clean and fresh smelling sheets on the antique bed in Aunt Anna's guest room — to sleep and wake up and find that those ten days never really happened.

When I woke up several hours later, the urgent matters weighed heavy upon me. One of the most pressing was to obtain a change of clothing and some money, but I was still afraid to go to my home or office — even with a bodyguard. However, after a quick breakfast to help replenish my strength, I decided to risk telephoning my home. It was early. Luci, my maid who had worked for me four years, would hopefully be up. I had already decided to hang up if someone else answered.

Luci did answer. She seemed surprised to hear my voice. Like Aunt Anna, she had been told by Zelda that I had gone to Acapulco for an extended vacation. She lowered her voice to a whisper: "Miss Petti, do be careful. Zelda and Johnny (Zelda's grown son) and some other people are living right here in your home!"

I tried to give a few-sentences version of what had happened to me, then I asked her to fill a small suitcase with a complete change of clothing, the money from my petty cash drawer, and my corporate checkbooks. I instructed her to take the case to the Shamrock Hotel, just a few blocks from my penthouse. The Shamrock doorman was a good friend; I knew he would be glad to hold the suitcase for me until I could pick it up.

Little did I know that my conversation with Luci had been tapped.

I needed medical attention, but I knew there were a few other more important items first.

Utmost on the list was a call to Dr. Le Roy.

He was a psychiatrist who worked with individuals who came with special needs to the Maritronics office. He also held group therapy sessions in connection with the diet-control center.

I didn't really know where to start unraveling the strange happenings, but I felt like Dr. Le Roy would know exactly what to do.

I briefly recounted my ordeal, then asked for his help: "Before this is all over, I might have to prove my sanity to someone, and that proof might also be useful in legal action against my kidnappers." Quite frankly, in spite of God's reassurances about my sanity, I still had nagging doubts. The ten days seemed so unreal. I felt that a psychiatric evaluation might help convince *me* that I hadn't *dreamed* everything.

Full of concern, Dr. Le Roy agreed to administer sanity clearance tests immediately.

Poor Aunt Anna. I had dropped in like a ragged waif a few hours previously. She was so worried as I prepared to leave. More than anything, she was fearful for my life.

"I've got to get this all cleared up today," I told her. "I will see you just as soon as this mess is figured out."

Officer Johnson willingly drove me to the psychiatrist's office. Dr. Le Roy was shocked to see me, more concerned about my physical appearance than anything, But I had too much to do before I got medical attention.

After administering the tests, Dr. Le Roy gave me the document I might need. He also put me in touch with his law office, since my own personal attorney, accompanied by his beautiful wife whom he met through Maritronics, had just left Houston to take a job with a Saudi Arabian oil firm. I hadn't needed anyone's legal services since he departed — until then.

We drove quickly and met a member of that law firm. I initiated legal action against my kidnappers. Though

LE ROY, M.D.

March 19, 1971

RE; Dr Petti Wagner

To Whom it May Concern,

I have examined Dr. Petti Wagner on March 19, 1971. In
my opinion she is not a danger to herself or others. She
has been through an unbeleivable amount of Torture and Trauma,
but in spite of this , she is mentally Sound by all Mental
Health Codes in the State of Texas. In my opinion she does
not need Psychiatric care now nor has she ever in the past
ten years I have know her and seen her almost daily in
business.
I am sending her to her own Physician for the very serious
injuries to her left eye and jaws.

Le Roy, M.D.

LE ROY, M.D.

August 30, 1971

                                        Re: Petti Wagner

To Whom It May Concern:

Petti Wagner is mentally competent to conduct her business and handle her own affairs.

LeRoy, M.D.

I hardly knew who to name, I had to protect my rights, personal and corporate, under the law.

Feeling better, I asked the officer to take me to the Shamrock Hotel to pick up my suitcase. There was so much more to be done that day, but I could hardly wait to change my clothes. Officer Johnson obediently headed his car towards the hotel, but warned me, "Dr. Wagner, even with as little as I know about all this, I don't believe I'd go there. Someone's out to kill you, remember?"

"But I've *got* to pick up my suitcase," I replied. "I want to make sure the checkbooks are okay. I need some cash in hand in case I have to stay away from my home tonight. And I definitely need those clothes."

He was silent, so I continued, "Plus, I can't run anymore. If I do, there'll never be an end to it. Whatever I'm up against, I've got to face it head on. Today!"

Officer Johnson promised to stand by me, even if we did encounter problems.

In just a few minutes, we were pulling into the drive that led to the hotel's registration area. Officer Johnson stopped the car and went inside to pick up my suitcase.

Then, as I sat waiting for him to return, a flash of ice water splashed through my brain. Johnny (Zelda's nineteen-year-old son) and four unfamiliar-looking men were approaching me. Johnny rushed ahead of the rest. He was unkempt, his dark, bushy hair ringing an animal-like face.

"Wagner," he sneered. "We caught you, didn't we?"

"Caught me?" I thought, alarmed. "What does he mean by that?"

"We have a warrant for your arrest," he boasted. The car window was opened enough that I could hear his snarling voice. "The sheriff will come to get you as soon as we tell him you've arrived here?"

"Arrived here?" How did he know I was going to be at

the Shamrock Hotel?

I tried to remain calm. Thankfully, Johnny and his companions backed away from the car. They saw Officer Johnson coming out of the hotel with a suitcase in hand.

"We'll notify the sheriff ourselves," I called out to the men as they fled.

I asked Officer Johnson to go back into the hotel to call the sheriff, then I made sure the car doors were locked and opened the suitcase. It was empty! No clothing. No money. No checkbooks. The suitcase wasn't even my own. I ached with despair. I knew my faithful Luci wouldn't betray me. Or would she? Or maybe Zelda had eavesdropped on the telephone call I'd made.

"That must be it!" I thought. "Luci could never..." My mind whirred. I wondered if I could trust anyone again.

Officer Johnson returned, his face etched with concern.

"There really is a warrant out for you, Dr. Wagner," he exclaimed. "Someone is claiming that you are mentally ill, and that you've escaped from custody which was essential for your protection and the protection of the community."

It sounded so official. Mentally ill? Protection of community?

"I-I'm sorry," he continued urgently, "I know that you are sane. The psychiatrist knows you are, too. But the sheriff has to do his job."

"But who?" I asked incredulously.

Then came the final blow.

"Peter Wagner," the officer stated flatly.

"*Not my own son!*"

I thought my heart would burst. We had always had a good relationship, though he had become more distant during the past year — not that unusual for most older adolescents. Still, I knew Peter would never do a thing like that. To my knowledge, I had never given any basis for anyone, certainly not my own son, to want me committed to a mental institution. That was absurd!

It had to mean that someone must have him under control, also. Maybe he was being held, too, as I had been. Or threatened with death.

"Lord," I breathed forcibly, "please take care of Peter — wherever he is."

I knew what I had to do.

"Let's go," I instructed my bodyguard. "Let's go right to the sheriff's office." I had always been more of a lover than a fighter, but I could spar with the best. This challenge had to be faced, and a jolt of adrenalin rushed through me. "We'll get this cleared up right away."

Unfortunately, at the Harris County Sheriff's Office, the cloudy situation became more shadowy, more threatening. The sheriff let us know that he was just doing his job.

"But I've been with Dr. Wagner since early this morning," my bodyguard affirmed. "She's not mentally ill! She even has an official statement from a psychiatrist to prove it. Look!"

The sheriff seemed perplexed. He was amiable, very clean-cut. He had an honest-looking face, but seemed determined to carry out the terms of my arrest.

"You can see that she's been horribly injured by somebody in that hospital," Officer Johnson continued emphatically. "Hey! She's here of her own free will. Does that sound like somebody who needs to be locked up?"

"That may be so," the sheriff barked, "but I've gotta go ahead with it. She's gotta be examined by one of the county psychiatrists before I can even satisfy the warrant. Then we'll see. It's outta my hands."

Despite Officer Johnson's protests, I was taken into custody then and there. I was still confident that everything would quickly be cleared up, and I asked Officer

Johnson to stay there. I would need him to resume bodyguard duties in a few moments when I returned from the nearby county hospital.

I had heard of many people who had been taken into custody, though quite sane, and detained for long periods of time under horrible situations. In most states, all it takes is a disgruntled relative and a willing (or paid-off) doctor. I had dealt with many such people who had been incarcerated unjustly (many of Dr. Holmes' electroshock patients were blatant examples of tragic loopholes in the state mental health codes). I just never imagined it happening to me. Like most Americans, I had felt so safe within the system. I never realized what it would really be like to be detained unwillingly, to be stepped on by that system — until then.

I was totally stricken with unbelief as the sheriff rushed me to the county hospital and ushered me up the elevator to the tenth-floor psychiatric ward.

The most difficult part was the absurdity of it all. I was hurt beyond description (though much of that first night's beating and kicking had started healing during those ten days — most of the final beatings had been with those leather-covered paddles on my buttocks and legs). Still, my face and fingers were quite bruised. My left eye was especially gruesome and swollen. The bath at Aunt Anna's had helped make me somewhat presentable, at least, but I couldn't understand why there was so much more concern about legal technicalities than about my health.

Of course, I had to admit, I had been the one who wanted "first things first." I had wanted to get my affairs back in order, then take care of my personal needs.

Still, I wasn't ready for what awaited me on the tenth floor.

When I handed Dr. Le Roy's sanity clearance to Dr.

Barnes, one of the psychiatrists at the county hospital, he merely glanced over it, tore it apart, and dropped it into the nearest wastebasket (thankfully, Dr. Le Roy's normal procedure was to make copies of all documents). That then-familiar sickening churn rose in my stomach. The doctor was obviously used to dealing with many different types of people, but he shocked me with his insensitivity.

"Can this really be happening?" I wondered fearfully. "To me?"

A nurse took me to a room and stripped me of the black outfit I had been wearing for eleven days (at least it was clean — thanks to Aunt Anna). She gave me a green hospital gown. I assumed it was for a useful purpose, at least. Perhaps I would be given a medical examination and my injuries treated.

Incredibly, no medical examination was made. I became suspicious but wasn't even allowed a phone call to a lawyer. I was taken immediately to a drab-looking room with eight bunks inside.

"How long will I be here before I get some medical help?" I asked, but the nurse gave no answer. The door clicked (Oh God, how I had come to hate that sound!), and once again, I seemed locked inside a morbid, absurd world.

There were several women there, and I was astonished to see someone I knew. Gert, a sallow-blonde wisp, had once been a tenant in one of the apartment buildings on my Houston property. Her life-style had so disgusted me — married to one man, living with another; an alcoholic — that when she repeatedly was unable to pay her rent, I had evicted her with little remorse.

But, instead of spewing hatred, she came to me, hugged me as if I were a long-lost sister, and asked how I was — "Dr. Wagner, what are you, of all people, doing here in this place?"

I didn't even want to begin an explanation of the tragic comedy I hardly believed, so I countered by asking about her. She had voluntarily checked into the county hospital to overcome her worsening drinking habit.

The absurdity continued. My request to see my personal physician, Dr. John McGuire, was refused; and, when I persuaded a nurse to call my newly hired attorney, there was a mix-up because he had just left the law firm.

God seemed to know what I was going through. During the worst possible, most humiliating time of my life, Gert was my touch with my life before the travesty began. Even in the psychiatric ward, among dopers and psychotics, she was a friend. I found myself confiding in her and praying for her — a woman with whom I would have never associated previously. A lot of snobbishness and egotism were being dissolved — if nothing else.

Even so, I was still imprisoned. I thought I was accustomed to the problems of being caught between legalities in the court system, but I never was more aware that the rights of an individual, almost any individual, can be snatched away without warning.

If I had expected anything or if I had a history of mental problems or if there had been more of a warning that I was being forced into a dingy corner I could have been more prepared for the atrocities and dehumanizations.

When, on Monday morning, I still hadn't received any physical treatment, I finally convinced a ward nurse to telephone Dr. McGuire. She agreed, so I also asked for Dr. Le Roy and my newly hired attorney — if possible. The three men arrived a short time later.

As my longtime friend and physician examined me, took a blood sample, and began to apply superficial dressings to my wounds, I told the three men everything that had happened. Everything. Perhaps I was still hurt that no one had looked for me during those ten days. The days in the county hospital hadn't helped.

Then Dr. McGuire began recounting to me about Lana and his attempts to locate me, of his growing concern about the food poisoning:

"I went to the hospital, but the staff totally denied your presence. Your assistant, Zelda, kept telling everyone that you had gone to Acapulco, but there were too many unanswered questions. And to think that all the time you *were* there," he shook his head sadly, "suffering this."

"Don't blame yourself," I said, trying to smile. With those familiar faces around me, I was beginning to feel courageous again. "It's all over now. As soon as the authorities can have their hearing this morning and pronounce me sane, I'll be out of here and we can get everything all cleared up."

It wasn't going to be quite that simple.

The Monday morning hearing was to determine whether or not I was sane and could be released without fear of injury to myself and others.

The man who presided over the hearing completed the formalities in five minutes. Since it wasn't a courtroom trial, Dr. McGuire and Dr. Le Roy were not permitted to offer testimony in my behalf, and neither my attorney nor I were allowed to say a single word in my defense.

The two hospital psychiatrists — Dr. Bates and the Dr. Barnes who had thrown away Dr. Le Roy's sanity clearance — both testified similarly — that they had examined me and found me to be mentally ill and in need of psychiatric treatment.

I couldn't believe my ears! Neither man had examined me! It was obvious that I was just another speck on the crowded parade of justice.

At the conclusion, after all had been duly considered (all five minutes), I was "sentenced" to be hospitalized and treated for an indefinite period.

Then I was offered a choice of care facilities: "You may elect to be taken to the state hospital in Austin," he began, "or..." I shuddered, knowing the reputation of the psychiatric department there. "Or," the man continued, "you may elect to be transferred to Houston General under the supervision of the court and pay your own bill."

I could see the wheels moving in Dr. McGuire's head. He was powerless, at the moment, to do anything about the "sentence," so he recommended that I sign the papers requesting an immediate transfer to Houston General.

"Petti," he whispered, "Dr. Le Roy and I can personally supervise everything there. We can get a court order forbidding the county psychiatrists to have anything to do with you. At least we can start working on finding out who is behind all this. When we do that, then we can start making some sense out of it."

Dr. Le Roy agreed, as did the young lawyer, so I signed my name. I was a prisoner, of sorts, again. I thought things like this only happened in psycho-suspense movies. Would it ever end?

JOHN O. McGUIRE, M.D.
2701 BERRY ROAD
HOUSTON TEXAS 77016

OX 5 6476

May 20, 1971

Dr. Olive P. Wagner
2223 Dorrington Street
Houston, Texas 77025

Dear Dr. Wagner:

As per your request, I am forwarding you this information. On March 6, 1971,
I examined you in my office. The examination was entirely within normal
limits with the exception of a slight pharyngitis and bronchitis, for which
I prescribed medication.

Yours truly,

John O. McGuire M. D.
John O. McGuire, M.D.

JOHN O. McGUIRE, M.D.
2701 BERRY ROAD
HOUSTON. TEXAS 77016

Dr. Olive P. Wagner
2223 Dorrington
Houston, Texas 77025

CHAPTER 14

Devastation

Though it seemed a horrible sentence, going to Houston General at least allowed me to receive the extensive medical attention I needed. Dr. McGuire had treated the worst problems, but I needed specialists.

My loft eye was cleansed and treated daily with compresses. The open wounds on my knees, legs, and hands were cleansed before being closed with tape, clamps, and stitches. The tendons of two fingers had to be surgically repaired. Penicillin was administered to combat infection.

I was a mess, even after the time which had elapsed. Every day I was immersed in a large tub of hot water to prevent the formation of blood clots in the damaged blood vessels. Four or five times each day the nurses put hot sand packs on me to speed the elimination of the various drugs which had accumulated in my body.

Some other fears were realized. Neither ear had worked well since that first beating. The ear specialists found that my right eardrum was ruptured and irreparable. The left eardrum had a smaller hole, so surgery was scheduled. A minute patch was put over the drum as a bridge to support the fragile tissue the doctor hoped would develop there.

A dentist was called in to see what could be done about my teeth, all of which were loosened (in varying degrees). Two were beyond saving, the doctor said, and all the others would have to be reset and supported. Sometime soon my mouth would require major reconstructive surgery.

One blow came after the next, but at least I was safe and cared for. Dr. Le Roy and Dr. McGuire, as they had promised, supervised the evaluation and treatment. Dr. Barnes and Dr. Bates, the county-appointed psychiatrists, were kept away from me by a court order obtained by the lawyer (funny thing, though, I would later receive an incredibly large bill from them for services rendered!).

After a week of recuperation, even though I was still supposed to be "sentenced" to Houston General, I was granted permission to leave the hospital to begin clearing away the gathering corporate clouds. At first I was able to be gone for three or four hours. Within another week the time increased.

As the story about me got out, family and friends thronged around to support me. Kimberli had also been told the "Acapulco" account, but when she heard the truth she came home from school to be with me. She was eighteen then, a senior in high school, so beautiful and alive and caring. Her flowing brown hair and large, expressive eyes brought such sunshine into my room.

Several of my sisters, who were scattered across the country, flew in from their homes. We were all very proud; I would have never asked them for money or help, but their mere presence meant more than anything else they could have done.

Kimberli and my sisters accompanied me on my first visit to the building which housed my home and my office. Also, since we still didn't know what might greet us there, we took along a policeman for protection.

I was thankful to have my family along to give me moral support that day, but nothing could have prepared me for the devastation I found.

Virtually everything was stripped from my Maritronics offices! Priceless antiques from Europe, desks, chairs, pictures — almost everything. I felt ravaged.

One broken desk that had been too large to go through the door — that was left behind. One little gold-leaf table still remained, smashed to bits. Fragments of picture frames were in disarray.

Room by room, we walked together surveying the horror. We did find the files of my Maritronics clients, obviously too heavy to move easily.

The walk through my penthouse was the same sad story. My closets were empty. Each year I had purchased a new wardrobe from Neiman-Marcus and gave away the old. The black pantsuit I had been wearing when I made that fateful visit to Room 120 was all that remained. My furs were missing except for one mink coat (my name had been specially imprinted on each pelt, so it would have been difficult to fence). Nearly a million dollars worth of jewelry was gone (including the pieces I had been wearing). Five sets of sterling silver, my beautiful Dresden china — the accumulations of a lifetime had vanished. Even the furniture and keepsakes up in the attic, which I had been saving for my children, had been taken.

I walked through the empty rooms like a zombie. Every time I had thought that nothing would shock or surprise me again, I would be shattered with yet another jolting revelation.

I wanted to believe that there was an end in sight,

that everything would work out, but it all seemed so futile.

My place, I was told, had been like one glorious grab bag. Neighbors said there had been a continual hauling away from the time I had "gone to Acapulco." In fact, the last truckload of desks and furniture had been taken from my home and office on Saturday, March 20 — the day after my leap to freedom — while I was being detained at the county hospital. The neighbors had assumed, quite naturally, that since Zelda seemed to be directing things, I had authorized the removal of my property to some other location.

Too many crises were coming to me too quickly. I still had little idea what I was facing. I didn't know yet if it were just a crazy set of scattered criminal acts against me or if it were some large conspiracy that included people, as it appeared, from my office workers to some of Houston's well-known elected officials. I was distraught and physically weak. I still had lots of fight in me, though, and I just wanted to start getting things back to normal.

Still, there was no word from Peter. All our efforts to locate him were unsuccessful. He had simply disappeared from college. Zelda, I was sure, could have told us where he was, but — like Peter — she had also dropped out of sight.

"My son, my son," I prayed. "Please help him, Lord, wherever he is."

Even in the midst of my frantic anxiety and continued shock waves, I remained acutely aware of Jesus' love. It was the constant I could cling to. I discovered a little chapel room in Houston General, and from the Bible there I read, "We are troubled on every side, yet not distressed; we are perplexed, but not in despair; Persecuted, but not forsaken; cast down, but not destroyed," (II Corinthians 4:8-9).

Scriptures like those were like new friends. I had

never known how personal the Bible could be, and, like a starving person suddenly being fed, I spent a lot of time in the chapel reading the Word of God. I had heard the Twenty-third Psalm quoted like a dusty poem lots of times before, but that passage became a lifeline to me — "The Lord is my shepherd; I shall not want...." I memorized the words of comfort so I could take them with me wherever I went.

Meanwhile, Dr. Le Roy and a police officer who had been a client of mine were conducting an investigation. My sister Shirley had been doing some snooping around my all-but-demolished office. Dr. McGuire, who — interestingly enough — had been a Texas Ranger before he became a physician, joined the impromptu detective work.

I knew the truth would have to come out, no matter how traumatic the knowledge might be. Then, I hoped, I could begin to piece things together and act accordingly. But after seeing the devastation in my home, and with all that had happened to me already, I was almost afraid to listen to the preliminary findings.

It hadn't taken my family and friends long to discover bits and pieces of a diabolical picture. Quickly, they meshed together information gleaned from talking to people involved, interviews with others, airport logs, carbon copies of letters, cancelled checks, records of phone calls, and bills Zelda and her people (whoever they were) never expected anyone to find.

It was such a twisted, tangled web — so outrageous and so bizarre that it sounded like the plot for a seamy paperback novel.

And the very worst was yet to come.

CHAPTER 15

Wine Of Hatred, Taste Of Greed

As soon as I disappeared, my friends and family learned, Zelda took complete control of everything. She was not the total instigator of the plot, nor was she the total "muscle," but she worked out the moves to make.

Why? She had much to gain, and little to lose. Zelda's private life was marred by two major problems. I had been completely unaware of either (and had no reason to know).

She used drugs, principally marijuana, on which she became increasingly dependent. It hadn't affected her work in the office (or had it?), but the growing reliance on the "weed" made her an easy, willing mark.

She had also fallen for a married man who was deeply in debt — the David for whom I prayed the night of my escape. While manager of a health club, he had borrowed $100,000 from the bank, hoping to make a quick fortune on a questionable investment in his company's stock. The owner of the company was a high roller, and when the investments reached a certain level, the owner pulled out his own inflated investment; the stock's value plummeted, and the other investors were left holding the proverbial bag (and a ragged, worthless bag to boot!). Instead of raking in the promised profits, David suddenly found himself staring at the payments on a hundred-grand note.

Her need for him and his need for money was the basis for everything to follow. By then, Zelda had ready access to the records of my corporations and to my bank accounts, annuities, insurance policies, medical records, etc. When her "sugar daddy" suddenly needed money to pay off the bank note, one-plus-one equalled me. I was the logical source.

The initial withdrawals apparently were accomplished by simple maneuvering of funds and through forging my signature. That helped with the bank note problem, but something must have clicked. If it were that easy, why not get more? This sort of thing happens in corporations, even banks, all the time throughout America and often goes undetected for weeks or months. If it is planned well, especially through today's computer systems, the genius embezzlers sometimes never get caught.

David and Zelda's mistake was the oldest in the book — they got greedy. Too greedy. My assets became the pot of gold. I just happened to be in the way.

Zelda and David apparently decided to take care of that incidental fact and charted a simple course of action. On November 18, 1970, they took out a $100,000 insurance policy on me naming Zelda as beneficiary (it's quite typical in the corporate world for one "officer" to name another officer, and can be easily effected).

Then Zelda began lacing my food with a slow-acting

poison (ample doses were found in my blood from the samples taken at the county hospital). That started sometime before Christmas. Because Zelda supervised the preparation of all the meals, mine included, there was little fear of detection as she administered the poison to me.

As the plot became more complicated (though we never could find when my son became involved), my regular employees were gradually discharged and replaced by persons who had no loyalty to me. This happened over a six-month period. I was too trusting of Zelda, true, but I had no reason to mistrust her. She had proven that she could handle the nuts-and-bolts of the business. I knew it was unusual for such a turn-over rate, but I had no contact with those former employees when they suddenly left (some, we found, were forced out; others were simply paid a "get lost" fee).

Anyway, one of the new employees, an accountant, forged my signature on letters to be mailed out after my death — each cancelling my substantial health insurance policies. Other letters with forged signatures began withdrawing annuities which I held (my sister discovered the annuity scam when she found carbon copies of the accountant's letters in the bottom drawer of the broken desk left in my office).

After New Year's Day (when I stopped eating the prepared meals for a short time), it must have been decided that I wasn't dying quickly enough. An increase in the daily dosage of poison in my meals could have caused the alarming symptoms that sent me to see Dr. McGuire.

It was no doubt during late 1970 and early 1971 that the kidnapping plot was hatched. The insurance policy reflects that it was ordered as early as November 1970, even though the delivery date was January 1971. Dr. Ronald Holmes agreed to superintend my "treatment" (he was contacted because of his notorious reputation) — and that treatment would put a small fortune in psychiatric fees into his coffers. He also eventually signed my death certificate so that the other financial pieces of the mystery could be effected. For this, he would collect his large bill from my health insurance companies, and he would receive $10,000 for my death certificate.

George and Don (I was told to pray for them during those pre-escape hours) were brought in to help David take care of all the details.

Everyone involved would make varying degrees of money, and my estate would be stripped bare.

From the moment I was safely locked up in Room 120, Zelda gained illegal control of my finances. In order to deplete my Maritronics and clinic accounts, she forged my name on checks and took them to Edna, her friend who worked in the bank where I did business. Edna had a price, too, but there was a deeper motive in her helping — I had once been forced to have an eviction notice served on her when she lived in an apartment I owned. I was the "cruel landlord" up in my "ivory tower" who disapproved of her cohabitation, so she easily played into Zelda's plans. Without checking with me or bank officers, Edna illegally issued cashier's checks to Zelda for the total amount held in my corporate accounts.

With the cashier's checks, Zelda opened new corporate accounts in another bank and listed herself as the only officer authorized to sign checks. In that way, Zelda and David not only gained control of my liquid assets, but also could tap into the funds flowing into the corporations. Admittedly, Zelda and David did their homework; still, it took a lot of daring.

With all the heady successes came momentum. To seize complete control of my real estate, the thieves needed very special help.

In fact, nearly everything Zelda and David were doing needed special cooperation of a family member. Exactly when Peter became involved is unclear, but various papers found in the Maritronics office indicated that Zelda had done a thorough job in convincing my son that I had lost my mind — that it was his duty to leave school immediately in order to take over all my businesses.

Quite frankly, if I would have had the proper relationship with my son, that part of the scheme probably wouldn't have worked. But while I was working to provide for my family, he had been placed in the finest military schools. He seemed to be happy and well-rounded, but I didn't know that my divorce from his father and subsequent separation from me as he progressed in his schooling — everything became a growing foment of resentment and rebellion.

When Zelda befriended Peter, she also involved him in the fast-paced world of drugs, impairing Peter's reasoning ability. He felt a growing sense of power. What he didn't realize was that he was getting dangerously involved with an increasingly high-stakes game.

There was no reason for Peter not to trust Zelda implicitly. He knew how thoroughly I relied on her. She also convinced him that I was socializing with people who were influencing me to make bad business maneuvers (not true).

It must have been an easy matter, therefore, for her to persuade him to sign documents casting doubt on my mental competence. And when a cooperative judge removed barriers which should have been raised by Peter's age, he was given full power of attorney over all my assets.

In Texas, like most states, an accusation of insanity leveled by one family member against another, no matter how false or unprovable, carries a ponderous weight. It can be one of the worst examples of "guilty until proven innocent," and sometimes allows a complete travesty of justice to occur. There is little means of protection when planned carefully enough. Surprise is a potent weapon when used properly. Zelda was a thorough planner. There were few hitches.

With Peter under their control and me locked away in Room 120, the kidnappers' greed ran rampant. They contacted tenants of my apartment building and generously offered to rewrite their leasing agreements. In exchange for large sums of cash, the tenants were given new two-year contracts at substantially reduced rents.

At the same time, my deeds were stolen from my safe in the office so the conspirators could start completing negotiations for the sale of my property. With me slated to disappear, no one would ever find out. A dead person cannot point fingers!

Everything went as planned. On March 18, the fatal shock treatment was administered, and all the final triggers began snapping. Dr. Holmes signed the death certificate.

Zelda's boyfriend, David, a braggadocious name-dropper with big dreams, was the first person the people at the hospital attempted to contact. David's main assignment then was to bring the final $5,000 payoff to Dr. Holmes for inking his signature, then David was to dispose of my body.

But David couldn't be reached at first — that was the delay, the reason why my body was left in Room 120 for those hours. He had flown to Florida in his twin-engine plane to hide moneys collected from my annuities and the sale of my buildings.

Upon his return, David was forced to land his plane at Houston International Airport because of poor weather conditions, but he still had one hour's flying time of fuel — enough to fly to Andreau Airport where the plane was always hangared and near the hospital where I was being held.

When David and his partner — a former attorney who had been disbarred by the state of Florida — finally received the message that I had died, it was late that day. David rushed to the plane with Dr. Holmes' payoff. The big-money time had arrived for them. He was naturally eager to pick up my body and the death certificate. Just the insurance policy alone meant $100,000 cash!

Then, an unusual string of occurrences started unfolding. David was unaware that his partner had already used the twin-engine aircraft that evening, flying somewhere one hour away to another location to hide other money *he* had collected. Because the attorney neglected to inform him, David thought he still had that hour's fuel in the tank when he and Theodore climbed into the plane; and in his hurry, he neglected to make the routine pre-flight check. Had he done so, he would have realized the plane was dangerously low on fuel.

After only a few minutes in the air, the engines of the plane stalled. David and Theodore plunged down into the Graves Sand Pit in woods near Humble, Texas. At that exact moment, one o'clock in the morning, God had me pray for David.

Details of the crash were headlined, AIR CRASH LEAVES TWO DEAD IN MONTGOMERY WOODS. Investigators found $5,000 in cash in the wreckage.

When David failed to arrive at the hospital on time, Dr. Holmes became impatient. Anxious to collect his money and "wash his hands" of the sleazy (but profitable) ordeal, he had his nurse call George, a man who had worked with me on a recent medical project. George, like David, was away from the telephone and unavailable for many hours.

George, an alcoholic (reformed, I thought), with thick glasses and a Master's Degree in Biology, had been cruising around Houston in an expensive car purchased with my money.

Late in the evening, judging by charges which later appeared on one of my horrendous credit card statements, he began to drink heavily. By the time Dr. Holmes' message got to him, George was quite drunk. With the doctor's payoff money in his pocket, he headed for the hospital on Westheimer Road.

He never made it. Just a few miles from the hospital he crashed into the back of a flatbed truck. The top of George's brand-new Cadillac was sheared away. Horrified witnesses were sickened as they saw a police officer on the scene carrying a man's head up the roadside embankment. Authorities found $5,000 cash on the decapitated body. Amazingly, the accident happened out on Highway 10 at two o'clock in the morning, the same time God told me to pray for the man!

When neither David nor George showed up at the hospital, Dr. Holmes' nurse put in a call to Don. I was surprised to find that Don, semi-retired from NASA, was already involved in the plot before I met him. Don's express purpose was to find out where I went in the evenings. I made no attempt to hide anything from him, and I listened on occasion as he talked about going into the ministry. He seemed like a fine addition to Maritronics. Little did I know.

But on the 18th of March, as he spent the evening with Dorothy Phillips, another member of Maritronics, his cocktail lounge chatter became compulsive. Suddenly he began blurting out everything he had done to hurt anyone — his ex-wife, his children, his ex-girlfriend. He even told Dorothy what he knew about the conspiracy against me, that he had received large payoffs for his role in keeping me under surveillance, that he was horribly sorry for what he had done.

Dorothy was very upset; and when she got home she spent several hours pacing the floor and praying for guidance. Was it true? If she reported him to the police, would she find that it was just a cruel joke? What should she do? She, too, had been told that I was vacationing in sunny Mexico. Not until after four in the morning did she finally muster the courage to call the police. By then, however, they already knew. I had just telephoned to hire a bodyguard!

Meanwhile, after Don returned home, he received the urgent message to bring the final payoff to the hospital. He jumped in his car and began driving toward Westheimer Road. He had just pulled onto a freeway when he suddenly began bleeding from his nose, mouth, and ears. In shock, he rushed himself to the nearest hospital. Records related that he was rushed into the intensive care unit. But it was too late. Don had been on blood-thinning medication for some time. He died of a cerebral hemorrhage at 2:45 a.m. precisely the time I was told to pray for him. On his person, hospital attendants found an envelope containing another $5,000 which Dr. Holmes would never see.

Before dawn on March 19th, four of the people responsible for the plot against me had died tragically and mysteriously — three for whom I had been told to pray while still in Room 120, and Theodore.

Although my guards had known of my extraordinary resurrection before six o'clock on Thursday evening (the 18th), the nurse had been unable to get back in touch with any of the three men who had been notified to pick up my body and bring the payoff to Dr. Holmes.

Friday morning, Steel-and-Thunder and the Follower awoke at eight, having fallen sound asleep in their chairs after the 9:20 p.m. flashlight check. Both of them had slept the night away, the only time since the first day of my imprisonment that one of them, at least, hadn't stormed into Room 120 several times during the night to flash the lights into my startled face.

By the time the guards checked my room, I had been gone nearly five hours. The escape was such an absurd, incredible impossibility. So utterly unthinkable to anyone! As the plotters heard of my resurrection and three-story-jump disappearance, they scrambled to cover their tracks. As soon as I called Luci, my maid, they realized that their only hope was to reiterate my insanity and have me reconfined immediately. Hence the warrant for my arrest.

Everything had gone so well for them until God and I started doing such unexpected, bizarre things. Coming back from the dead — that messed up all the timing. And the escape — that sent everyone scurrying to cover their suddenly exposed schemes.

And the deaths — that just added to the absurd craziness of what was happening. Those were just the beginning. Others would die, too.

It was coming too fast at me. Each new day, even after I was safe among friends and family, brought new revelations.

I had always been relatively protected. My daddy, my suitors, my college professors, my colleagues — all had helped keep me from the ugliness and hatred "out there." So much of my life had been wonderful and creative and profitable. There had been problems, but none I couldn't overcome. I had been self-reliant, to a fault. That had been my strength, but my strength had also become the greatest chink in my armor.

Almost everything I had held dear was taken from me. I had been stripped — personally or corporately — as devastatingly as had been my office and home.

Even my son had been taken. There had been no word about him.

Without Kimberli and my own family, it would have been impossible to go on.

I had lost everything. But I had found everything, too.

I had discovered what (and Who) was most important. My priorities had changed, were changing. Every day with my Lord became more dear. The faith I received from those incredible, unearthly hours with Him helped me hold onto all the promises I kept finding in His Word.

But I couldn't help wondering what lay ahead. Somehow, I had the feeling that the worst horrors were *yet* to come.

UNITED STATES DEPARTMENT OF JUSTICE

WASHINGTON, D.C. 20530

Address Reply to the
Division Indicated
and Refer to Initials and Number

Dr. Olive Peet Wagner
2223 Dorrington
Houston, Texas 77030

Dear Dr. Wagner:

President Nixon has referred to this department your letter of
May 1, 1971, Concerning your recent Kidnapping and torture ---
both mentally and physically and the Outrageous induction of
240 volts of electricity into your body. Be assured we are
giving this information our immediate attention.

You have set forth sufficient and specific information to enable
us to determine whether a violation of a federal statute is
involved. We should be able to come to an immediate conclusion
within a few days.

Please be assured this matter will receive our careful consideration
and that President Nixon is concerned and we will do everything in
our power to see that Justice is done.

                                Sincerely,

                        Assistant Attorney General
                        Civil Rights Division

U. S. DEPARTMENT OF JUSTICE
WASHINGTON, D. C. 20530

OFFICIAL BUSINESS
PENALTY FOR PRIVATE USE, $300

POSTAGE AND FEES PAID
U. S. DEPARTMENT OF JUSTICE
JUS-431

Dr. Olive Peet Wagner
2223 Dorrington
Houston, Texas   77025

May 18, 1971

Mr. Jack Reed
Firemans Fund
P. O. Box 664900
Houston, Texas 77006

Dear Mr. Reed:

Attorney Chuck Stepenson informed me today that you wanted ten (10) samples of my handwriting in both signatures Patti Wagner and Olive P. Wagner, President.

I also wish to inform you that the checks in question were written while I was in ▇▇▇ Hospital. I was there from March 8, 1971 to March 18, 1971. One of the checks was written out of the middle of the check book on March 9, 1971, in the amount of Eight thousand dollars ($8000) and the other check was written on March 15, 1971, in the amount of Nine thousand eight ($9800) dollars I was in ▇▇▇ Hospital without any communication with the outside world from March 8, 1971 to March 18, 1971. There was not any way that I could have written the above specified checks on or before these dates.

Other forgeries on this account amount to $22,500 during this period of time. My bookkeeper will vouch for the fact that I never took checks from the middle of the check book, nor did I ever sign any blank checks without having the complete amount and the same filled in with complete detail.

My bookkeeper never gave ▇▇▇ these checks from the middle of the check book nor did I. The only time ▇▇▇ had access to our check book was after I was placed in ▇▇▇ Hospital on March 8, 1971. I have not seen her again as of this date, although she moved into my office and took over until April 1, 1971.

SINCERELY IX.

Olive P. Wagner
Olive P. Wagner, President

First State Bank of Bellaire
5123 Bellaire Boulevard
Bellaire, Texas

January 11, 1972

Attention: Mr. Cook

Re: Mrs. Olive P. Wagner
    Diet Control Corporation

Dear Sir:

On November 8, 1971 I wrote you enclosing copies of forged checks in the amount of $24,404.11 which forged checks had depleted the account of my client, Olive P. Wagner and Diet Control Corporation. We have received no word from as to your intentions regarding this matter although we advised at the time that our client was making claim for same. We will appreciate if you will at once discover the status of this matter and advise us.

Yours truly,

Jerry J. Hamilton

JJH/rb
bcc: Mrs. Olive P. Wagner
     2223 Dorrington
     Houston, Texas

CHAPTER 16

Shekinah

For a total of twenty-two days, I spent my nights and at least part of every afternoon at the downtown hospital. It wasn't a bad arrangement at that point. I received physical therapy and care for my wounds; plus, it was the best and safest hotel accommodation for which I could ever have hoped.

Still reeling from the absolute horror of everything that had happened, I used my daily hours of leave from the hospital trying to restore Maritronics to some semblance of an operating business.

All my other buildings had been sold. Only the one which housed my apartment, the Maritronics office, and the diet kitchen still belonged to me; it had been in contract of sale and could not be touched.

Except for the broken desk, all the furniture was gone, but at least the Maritronics files were still intact.

The authorities, my friends, and family were helping me, but we could not find out who had bought my other properties, since the missing deeds had not yet been filed at the courthouse. We did know, however, that the furniture in the buildings which had been sold was still legally mine — unless that had been stolen, too. I hired a truck and a crew of men to find out. Since my keys had vanished with my pocketbook that first day of imprisonment, the men had to take the doors off the buildings to get inside. I wasn't surprised to learn that everything of real value in those buildings had disappeared, too. But with the few pieces of furniture which remained, I began refurbishing my office and home.

The mere fact that the hospital allowed me to come and go freely hardly pointed to my "danger to the community." In fact, my final release from the hospital was only delayed because Zelda had obtained Peter's signature in the first place. Zelda and the rest also stood to collect thousands of dollars for the added time I was hospitalized from accident and health policies.

My home was anything but a castle anymore. Suspecting that my house had been used as headquarters for a massive illegal drug operation during those fateful ten days, police had earlier conducted a thorough search there. In the attic, under the rafters, they uncovered large amounts of pure heroin which had obviously been overlooked during the hurried departure as the plot began to fall apart.

Even my white Cadillac convertible had been used for the drug operations. Credit card bills, which began pouring in, left a well-traveled track from Houston to Alice, Texas, and points between. When the police found the car abandoned, they took it to the garage and literally tore it apart. Traces of dope had triggered their search, and they found a small fortune of illegal substances in every conceivable hiding place.

I did get my Cadillac back, but it was never the same. The parts which had been removed by the police mechanics rattled and shook.

Because my home had been used as headquarters
for the kidnappers' drug operations during those days
I was imprisoned, attempted break-ins were frequent.
I was forced to build my "castle" into a virtual fortress.
All the windows were secured, and alarm systems
were installed throughout.

By the time I moved home, my sisters had returned
to their homes. Then, after Easter vacation, Kimberli
went back to school (though she returned each weekend). I did have police protection in the place — my
bodyguard and his German Shepherd dog watched
over me.

I was panicky. Jumpy. It was sheer terror for me to try
to sleep at night. Noises frightened me. Crowds. I asked
those close to me to approach me from the front, not
from the back or side. I still couldn't hear, except for
limited abilities in one ear.

Sometimes when I thought about the utter impossibility of all that had happened I would be almost
overwhelmed with confusion. In such moments it was
all I could do to hold tightly to God's promise: "You are
very much alive, and your sanity is insured by Me."

He kept bringing a Scripture to my mind — II Timothy
1:7: "For God hath not given us the spirit of fear; but of
power, and love, and of a sound mind." That verse
became a vital bedrock of my sanity. Everytime I started thinking, "That couldn't really have happened to
me," I could regain stability by claiming His promise.

Immediately following my return home I felt con-
strained to do something quite strange. Just as clearly
as He had instructed me in the escape, the Holy Spirit
prompted me every night to drive to the intersection of
Houston's Montrose and Drew Streets. I didn't know
why I was there, but I followed the leading of the Spirit,
drove to the corner, and worshipped God in the language He had given me. Then I also prayed in English,
asking God to watch over Kimberli at her school, and

over Peter, wherever he was — to bring him safely home. When I prayed for my son, God's answer was always the same: "If you never give up, I will not, either." Then He would remind me of another Scripture I had found, Acts 16:31 — "Believe on the Lord Jesus Christ, and thou shalt be saved, and thy house."

I had to count on that promise to work for my household, too. I felt that Peter's very life depended upon it.

Every morning, though I was never told why it was that specific time, the Holy Spirit began to come to me at three o'clock and teach me the Bible.

Because of the damage inflicted on my eyes, I couldn't read small print, not even out of the "good" eye, but by placing a lamp with two 150-watt bulbs next to my bed, I was able to read the verses I wrote in large block letters as He dictated them to me.

At the same time, God gave me spelling lessons. I had always been an adept speller, but the electrocution caused a noticeable loss of that ability.

As He dictated the verses to me, when I misspelled a word (which was often), He would stop me.

"You must not write over that word," He would say, "but draw a line through it. It represents one mistake you have made in your life. But remember, you can always start over. I have erased all your mistakes. I am restoring your soul."

He was so patient and precious with me, even when I wanted things to change quickly.

One of my greatest problems was my eyes. I had gone to see the specialist about my left eye, still swollen and useless. The doctor concluded that the eye was irreversibly damaged, and that I would never recover my sight! His recommendation was removal of the eyeball to protect the vision of my other eye. Perhaps it was a woman's vanity, but that seemed like a horrible sentence to me. It seemed so final.

However, I tried to accept such a fate. Every day I went to the hospital to have the socket treated in preparation for a glass implant. The intricate measurements were taken, the doctor's report was completed, and all the insurance paperwork was finished. Everything was in order for me to receive a cosmetically acceptable, but sightless glass eye.

Two days before the scheduled surgery, God woke me an hour later than usual.

"Get up!" He said. "Go down the hall and look at My picture."

I tiptoed quietly from my bedroom, hoping I wouldn't disturb the men or the dog downstairs. Following the Lord's instructions, I looked intently at the small Kriebel picture of Jesus which Kim bought me some time before. It was the only piece of art that hadn't been stolen from my home.

I looked at the picture for a few minutes, then I returned to my room and took up my note pad to record the day's instructions. I was still perplexed why I had been told to look at the picture, but I pushed it from my mind and wrote the time — 4 a.m.

In my excitement and puzzlement, I had neglected to close the door of my room.

Suddenly, I heard the Holy Spirit's voice coming through the open doorway — "Today I am going to take away the terror forever."

I looked up at a bright ball of light entering my room, the same brilliant orb which had filled Room 120 that night. From where I sat on my bed, I could see that the light was coming from the same area where I had stared at the picture of Jesus.

As before, the light split momentarily into three smaller masses, then the voice of the Father spoke: "I am the Lord thy God. I am here to help you and not to hurt you. Do not be afraid. We are all here — Father, Son, and Holy Spirit."

The brightness was so intense. It completely swallowed up the then-puny illumination of my two 150-watt bulbs. In the brilliance saturating everything in the room God showed me the army of angels He had sent for my protection. What he revealed was shocking! The entire ceiling was covered with beautiful faces.

Although some part of me remained seated on the bed and continued to write, at the same time I felt myself floating at the top of the room with the angels. Again, God was sharing with me His perspective of the whole universe.

For a brief instant I knew the end of events as well as the beginning and the middle. I could see it all working in perfect harmony. I was experiencing the same rush of unlimited knowledge as I had known in my heavenly encounter with the presence of Jesus. The peace was beyond my understanding! I saw a magnificent lion with a little lamb close beside. As before, a rosy glow enveloped the entire panorama.

My whole life passed before me. It was like a motion picture of myself — all I had done. I was amazed to see the way I had rushed about in a near frenzy, trying to learn and do and taste everything in the world all at once.

While I watched, Jesus pointed out to me that I had always been rushing through life. Many things had been good and beneficial — racing there to pay someone's tuition to school, flying there to arrange for a needy child to have surgery, dashing somewhere else to start a new business. Always rushing.

"What was all that about?" He asked gently. "Why have you been struggling so with life?"

"Lord," I said, the revelation washing through me, "there really is no need for such a struggle at all, is there? I have done many things right, but I've also been running after the wrong things, too. Is that why all this happened? I've been rushing about, but if I would only stop long enough to love You ..."

When I spoke those words, "to love You," a sensation like the outpouring of liquid love began warming me from the top of my head, spreading to the tips of my toes, washing through every cell of me, inside and out.

Then I saw the radiance condense and gradually diminish in size as it streamed back down the hallway.

I looked at the clock. 4:14 a.m. Then I realized that I was seeing with both eyes! With unblurred vision!

Hot tears brimmed, then spilled onto my cheeks. I ran from my bed screaming, "I CAN SEE! I CAN SEE! I CAN SEE!"

I turned on the light in the bathroom. Staring at me from the mirror was my face, but it was so different from the image I had seen during recent days.

The purple bruises were gone! The wrinkles from all the shock seemed smoother. My hair was still white, but in the socket of my once sightless, hopelessly injured left eye was a *perfect new one!*

My screaming had naturally set the German Shepherd downstairs to barking. The police and bodyguard bounded up the stairway. They didn't even recognize me at first; I could see it in their eyes.

But the dog knew me, all right. He had stopped barking when he saw me. His friendly tail was wagging.

Then I started laughing at the tenseness of the moment. That, more than anything, convinced them that I *was* Petti Wagner.

The men were as shocked as I was when I tried to relate what had happened. It seemed so mystical, so unbelievable. But none of us could ignore the fact that my face was healed. I could see with both eyes, and the swollen ugliness was completely gone. I could even hear better, though not perfectly yet.

I was still in such awe. I was overwhelmed with my

shortcomings, with my rushing around, with my neglect
of Him. Yet, God's love was all-forgiving, all-powerful. I
didn't feel I deserved all He had done, but I was still just
beginning to experience the depth of God's love. I was
also just starting to learn that God's peace consisted
of an absolute resignation to His will.

CHAPTER 17

Restoration

At ten o'clock the next morning I was still in bed,
writing down all the things God was saying to me.
Suddenly He told me, "I am going to restore everything the cankerworm and palmerworm have eaten."

I didn't know what that meant, or that it was also in
the Bible, but it sure sounded as if it covered a lot of
territory.

He had just taken care of my eye and healed all my
bruises. Even my damaged ears had been improved
during the night's visitation. But Peter was still missing. My teeth were loose. My mouth required major
surgical reconstruction. Every new day brought more
bills and more reports which showed more completely
that my businesses and finances were in shambles.

"Patience ... patience," I reminded myself. "Remember what you've learned. Rushing around and
churning inside isn't the best way to get things done.
You must learn to rest — to wait upon the Lord to do
these things for you."

As it happened, I didn't have long to wait before the next installment of His miracle-filled restoration.

First, though, I got dressed and went to the hospital to let the physicians confirm what God had done for me. The doctors and nurses there were amazed — not only that I could see with my once-sightless eye, but also that my face, so discolored with bruises, had also been completely healed.

I was still shaken by all that had happened as I sat at my desk later that day.

"Could I have just imagined that God said He was going to restore everything which had been taken from me?"

As if in answer to my unvoiced question, I was impressed to turn in my Bible to Joel 2:25. Amazing! There were the same words which God had spoken! He was confirming what he had told me; plus, I was actually reading from a Bible!

Then the telephone rang.

"Are you Dr. Petti Wagner?"

"Yes, I am."

"You are the one who lives on Dorrington?" the resonant voice asked.

"Yes, I am."

"Well," the man said, "I am Dr. Frazier, head of the periodontal department in the clinic just around the corner from you. I know this is going to sound crazy to you, but God woke me up at four o'clock this morning and gave me your telephone number. I checked it out and found you were only a couple of blocks from my office." Then he dropped the bombshell — "God says I am to do some reconstructive surgery on your mouth and the bones of your face!"

"You've been talking to the same God I have," I finally stammered, "and He has told me He will restore everything that's been destroyed."

He wanted me to come for my first consultation that

same afternoon. Naturally, he wanted to know how my mouth and teeth had gotten in such wretched condition. I told him the whole story. Instead of doubting, he let me know that he was doubly certain that God had called him to do the job. And before I left Dr. Frazier's office that day, he let me in on the real shocker — there wouldn't be any charge to me for his professional services! In fact, across my chart in bold letters, the doctor wrote, "No charge forever. Never!"

CHAPTER 18

Threads in the Tapestry

Calmly, see the mystic Weaver
   Throw His shuttle to and fro:
'Mid the noise and wild confusion,
   Well the Weaver seems to know
What each motion and commotion
   What each fusion and confusion
In the grand result will show.
                    —Unknown

Restoring my finances seemed an almost impossible task, despite what had transpired previously.

Before my kidnapping, I had unlimited credit at all the major department stores in Houston. I had credit cards from major gasoline companies. My pocketbook contained the American Express card, Diners Club, Carte Blanche. I used them sometimes, especially when I didn't want to carry the cash or a checkbook, or when I wanted to keep an accurate record. All that credit was hardly a status symbol. It was just something I used for convenience.

But in the aftermath, as the weeks and months progressed, the mail brought new disasters every day. All forms of bills reflected what a glorious shopping spree my enemies had enjoyed with my plastic money. It started the day I walked into Room 120.

Technically, I was only responsible for $50 on each card once I notified the individual companies. Unfortunately, it was many days before I *could* notify them.

The monthly statements showed enormous charges which I had never authorized. Zelda and the others must have gone on a wild shopping spree!

Huge expenditures showed up for food and drink, televisions, for stereos, pianos, organs, furniture, draperies. It looked as if someone had furnished an apartment at my expense.

Before long, the credit card charges totalled a staggering $89,000.

If I had charged that much, I wouldn't have batted an eye. I was accustomed to moving in a high-rolling world. But with all my tangible financial assets taken away, I didn't know how I could ever pay off those debts.

Still there was more. Much more. Bills which wouldn't have daunted me a month or two before loomed like an ominous weight.

At first, the most pressing financial problems were my telephone bills. When I returned to the office, all the phones had been disconnected. I contacted the telephone company to have service restored, but learned that I had nearly $4000 worth of long distance bills to pay first, thanks to my kidnappers! Deprived of the telephone service essential to my businesses, how could I ever pay anyone anything?

I was at the point of despair. Had God brought me so far, so quickly, to let me wallow in a rising tide of overpowering obligations.

I had several alternatives. I could have gone to any

of my brothers or sisters, but that was so unthinkable. We loved each other, but none of us had ever borrowed from the other. Never. So that was out of the question. I knew I would rather do without than to trouble family or friends.

No, it was just Jesus and me. He kept reminding me that we were not completely bankrupt, though some of His ways were humbling.

"Take your honor ring and pawn it," He said. "I will use the ring to put you back in business so that you can pay off all those bills."

Now that was strange to me. Why did I have to pawn it? Why not sell it? I knew I would probably only get a pittance. I didn't see how God could raise thousands of dollars by pawning one ring, but I had no other options available at the moment.

Having the ring removed was no problem. I simply went to Klarr's, my favorite jewelry store, in Greenbriar Plaza, just a block from my house. Mr. Klarr had made me many beautiful rings and other pieces of jewelry in the past. He knew about the kidnapping and had been invaluable in helping me list many of my stolen pieces. He easily cut off the ring which Tiffany's had made for me, but all the way back to my office, I grumbled about pawning it.

"God, I've never pawned anything before. Where do I go? What do I do?"

The answer was immediate: "Take it down to Dowling Street and pawn it for $500."

Five hundred dollars! That was nothing compared with what I owed to just the telephone company. Still, I was convinced that God had something out of the ordinary in mind.

Just as I walked back into my office at Maritronics, an old friend came in. I told him what I had been doing and why. He knew exactly what to do.

"Let me take your ring for you to Wolfe's on Dowling

Street," he offered.

My mouth fell open. I hadn't mentioned Dowling Street. Sure God was leading, I handed the ring to him.

A short time later, he returned. He dropped $500 and a claim ticket from Wolfe's. As he put the cash into my hand, I realized that I hadn't mentioned the amount to him, either. God was surely at work. (I did eventually get the ring back).

Before that day was over, I was at the telephone office with that $500, plus another $500 which I had borrowed from a Maritronics' client. The phone company accepted the $1000 as a down payment on what was owed, and full service was restored on the seventeen phones at Maritronics.

That same day, God dictated a letter for me to mail to all my creditors:

> **To whom it may concern:**
> Legally, I owe you nothing because the signatures you have on those credit purchases were forged. But I feel a moral obligation to you. God and I want to repay every dime. We will see that you receive your money with interest before a year has passed.
>
> (signed) Dr. Petti Wagner

As I typed the last words, "before a year has passed," my spirit felt relieved immensely. I knew the message had been dictated by God. Seeing the words on paper made me feel as if the debt had already been paid.

In the past, I had tackled many gigantic bills all by myself. I had been successful then. But to be able to have three able Associates to help me — the Father, Son, and Holy Spirit — that was terrific! Nothing God had directed me to do thus far had been even slightly off course. And, though I faltered, I was getting it more solidly settled in my spirit that when God made a promise, it was already accomplished in Eternity. All I had to do was watch the fulfillment unfold (and do my part, of course).

I sealed the letters and sent them off. I certainly didn't know how God was going to pay everything off, but He did. I had to have that kind of faith. God had proven over and over to me that He was real, and that He had a plan for the life He had restored to me when I had made the choice to finish my work on earth. He had been demonstrating to me that He was going before me to make the crooked paths straight. I was certain that I was surrounded by an army of angels since that night when He healed my eye.

After the telephones were reconnected and the letters in the mailbox, some pretty unusual things started happening.

The day after I mailed the letters, an elegant looking couple appeared at the door of my office. I didn't recognize them until they identified themselves.

"Petti," the man said, "I'm Jim Wells. This is Margaret. Do you remember?"

Then I *did* remember. I became acquainted with the Wells during the early Fifties. Jim had been a millionaire as head distributor for a popular vitamin and herbal product until he lost a battle with the FDA. During the court battle, he had lost everything, even his luxury car.

Not long after that happened, Jim came to my office to return some borrowed equipment. Deeply concerned over his unbelievably bad fortune, I went out to his old car to say goodbye to Margaret and their five children. One look at the pinched, woebegone faces utterly broke my heart. The car was in such sad condition and had four bald tires.

When I questioned them, they admitted that they had only a few dollars, hadn't eaten since the day before, and were headed to his brother's house in Abilene to make a fresh start.

I told Jim to wait a minute, ran back to my office, and

wrote out a check for $6000. The look in the faces of those five sweet children was worth more than the money.

Over the years, I had thought of Jim and Margaret Wells and wondered if they had ever made it to their destination in that old rattletrap of a car. I wasn't concerned about the money. In fact, so few people had ever returned the money I had loaned, that I had written most off as gifts. There was pleasure in that, too.

"God woke me up this morning," Jim explained, "and told me to come to Houston. He said I was to give you back twice what you had given us in 1952!"

He had used that $6000 check to buy necessities, then invested the rest in the food-freezer business. He and Margaret had become very successful. Then, when he won his battle with the government over the vitamin and mineral product, he had developed that into a thriving business all over the country.

That $12,000 was only the beginning. From every part of the country, people to whom I had made loans throughout the years began repaying me. I had forgotten most of them. It was mind-boggling how so many could have started repaying their loans at the same time.

In addition, with some advertising, Maritronics began doing a landslide business. Prospective clients who had been interviewed years earlier suddenly decided to pay their fees and join the organization.

Not that the picture was completely rosy. Everything didn't fall into place. I was still getting letters from tacky collectors. I dreaded to see what each day's mail would bring in, to see *what else* I owed. Only the envelopes with checks (accounts receivable and loan repayments) kept me in business.

Sometimes, despite everything God had done for me, I wondered how in the world I would handle the tidal waves coming against me.

It was like a million octopuses coming at me, the tentacles slithering in from all directions. I still didn't know who the real enemy was. We still hadn't found Zelda. Peter was still gone. What was still coming down? Were the doctors involved in other plots against me?

Though I looked worldly-wise and self-sufficient, I was very naive about life — not about people, but about life. I was one of nine daughters, and my father had always seen that we were well-chaperoned. We had been driven to parties and socials in limousines. Then, when I was married, I was protected by my husband. During the years since our divorce, I had been so well cared for by my staff (*too* protected, as it turned out).

I had handled making millions, and could do that well. But when all the horrible problems came at once, I knew I needed help to cope with all the technicalities being thrown at me. There was so much to be done. Plus, I had so little money to hire attorneys and detectives.

During the first month following my release from Houston General, especially after every day's mail brought word of new financial calamities, it became very obvious that I needed another attorney to represent me. The one I had hired in haste the first day after I escaped just wasn't working out.

But who was it to be?

"Jerry Hamilton," the Lord said one day. "Find Jerry Hamilton."

"Who is Jerry Hamilton?" I asked.

For thirty days the Lord repeated the man's name to me. No one around me seemed to know of such a man. I began to look everywhere. I even filled a legal pad with notes as I tried to track him down. The telephone was no help. The local bar association didn't have him on record. Someone with that name had once worked for a local bank, but no one knew his whereabouts.

I continued working at Maritronics, trying to make some semblance of my once successful business. But I also kept trying to find *that* Jerry Hamilton about whom the Lord kept telling me.

Finally I gave up. I had some pressing legal matters I had to start. I had to find an attorney. After interviewing three different firms, I decided to hire Campbell, Lilley, and Navarro. I was impressed with the way they talked, with their operating procedures, and with their honesty.

As for the name God had told me, well, perhaps I had missed His leading somewhere.

The day after I retained that firm, I was busy going over papers on my desk. I was startled to see two men. One was Mr. Campbell, whom I had hired. The other man was tall, slim, handsome, with the happiest, most peaceful face I had seen in some time. His eyes were friendly, and his ear-to-ear smile added to the warmth.

"Allow me to introduce our new partner," Mr. Campbell said. "He has just joined our firm today. He will be handling all your cases for you."

Mr. Campbell paused, glanced at the stranger, then back to me — "Dr. Wagner, meet Jerry Hamilton."

JERRY HAMILTON! The day after I had given up my search, God had delivered His handpicked man right to my office!

I grabbed my legal pad and handed it to the young man. It must have had "Jerry Hamilton" written a hundred times along with the dead-end notes.

"Read this," I urged. "I've looked everywhere for you."

He glanced at the yellow pad.

"Do you think God sent you?" I asked him.

"Yes," he said simply, "I know he did."

Actually, though he grew up in a Christian home, Jerry was not a serious Christian. I didn't know that when we met.

He became a special attorney and friend. From that day forward, I felt perfectly safe putting all my legal concerns into his capable hands. God had sent me a man who was wise, gentle, and honest — one who would help me in the gigantic, upcoming legal battles.

Neither of us knew the changes we would go through. Before long we would be facing an impossible task together. The results would alter both of us forever.

FLORIDA RESEARCH INSTITUTE
• • •
ADMINISTRATIVE OFFICE
State Chartered

March 11 1972

HONORIS CAUSA

We, the Faculty and Board of Directors of Florida Research Institute and the University of Florida have scheduled this Convocation in which we honor you, Dr. Olive Peet Wagner.

At this time, it is my pleasure to cite some of your accomplishments and your help to others.

Your research interests for the ultimate benefit of humanity are numerous, such as cyclo-therapy for crippled children, crippled children's clinics, studies in agriculture and medicine and other disciplines. Your psychological counseling service has helped both children and adults to a happy, wholesome life. Indeed, in many cases, you have been their inspiration. Your gifts to Stanford University and many other colleges in excess of $1,500,000 have paved the way for better education . . . a better life for many others. Indeed, Dr. Olive Peet Wagner, your love for your countrymen has been exemplified many times . . too many for us to mention at this time.

But, you have graced our colleges with your presence . . . releasing your time from your business activities in Houston to visit us. Your award is our pleasure. We believe God Eternal, your loyal friends including, of course, Florida Research Institute will forever be with you.

In fide et fortitudine, you have shown your courage and bravery in emerging victorious over the recent evils of your kidnapping. For that reason alone, Dr. Olive Peet Wagner, we are most happy to confer on you our Highest Honorary awards - - The Honorary Doctor of Letters and Psychology Degree!.

President

Faculty Representative

Board Representative

CHAPTER 19

Crash Course

Just three days after I received my new eye, I ran into Melle, a dear friend who taught art at a public school. She was literally glowing, almost in the same way I beamed after my visit to heaven.

I told her, as we talked briefly, some of what had happened to me. I also wanted to know why she looked so happy.

Well, she hadn't died, as I had. She told me she had experienced what she called "the baptism in the Holy Spirit."

At a prayer meeting, Melle told me, someone had asked her if she had received "the promise of the Father" after she became a believer. She found that it was the same question Paul asked the Christians in Ephesus nearly two thousand years ago (Acts 19:2). When Melle told that person, just as the Ephesians told Paul, that she hadn't even heard of such a thing, her questioner did for her what Paul did for the believers at Ephesus: he laid hands on her, and she was immediately baptized in the Holy Spirit and spoke in other tongues.

As we talked, Melle opened a Bible and showed me several Scriptures about speaking in tongues and about the baptism in the Holy Spirit. I was surprised to hear about so many references. I wondered why I had never heard about it in church.

"Every one of the Gospels mentions this baptism and speaks of Jesus as the One who baptizes in the Holy Spirit," she explained.

As we talked, I realized that the baptism was what had happened to me when I was in heaven with Jesus. The strange syllables I heard myself saying, after I returned to my earthly body, were examples of the "other tongues" mentioned so often in the Book of Acts. The Apostle Paul, who thanked God that he spoke more in tongues than anyone else, highly recommended them, (I Corinthians 14:18).

Melle then explained that in giving me English words to pray immediately after that experience, the Holy Spirit had been interpreting the other tongues for me.

I was fascinated. Maybe I was more relieved than anything to find that I wasn't the only one in the world (besides those "Holy Rollers" back in Iowa) who prayed like that! And I was glad to know that the prayers I had been lifting up every night at the corner of Montrose and Drew Streets were instances of the Holy Spirit's perfect intercession through me for Peter.

I was intrigued. Before we parted, Melle invited me to go to her church the next Sunday.

"We can have dinner together afterward," she added, "and talk more about all this."

I did. We did. And after we finished that delicious meal, Melle handed me a present — a copy of *The New English Bible.* It was an easy-to-understand, modern translation, just the thing for someone not schooled in the Word.

I related to that Bible so well. I had never really
studied before as I did with Melle's gift. I started mark-
ing in the margins, underlining special passages, even
writing my own "Ten Commandments" in the back.

But there was one majestic message He spoke which
reached into my deepest hurt.

"You have been asking, 'Why?'" He said. "You have
wondered what it was all about, and why those awful
things happened to you. Turn to Revelation 2:7-11,
and I will show you that I have written your life in My
book."

I opened to the passage He named. The words had
been written thousands of years before, but they were
exactly for me.

> "To him who is victorious I will give the right to eat from the
> tree of life that stands in the Garden of God . . . These are the
> words of the First and the Last, who was dead and came to
> life again: I know how hard pressed you are, and poor, and yet
> you are rich; I know how you are slandered . . . Do not be
> afraid of the suffering to come. The Devil will throw some of
> you into prison, to put you to the test; and for ten days you will
> suffer cruelly. Only be faithful till death, and I will give you the
> crown of life. Hear, you who have ears to hear, what the Spirit
> says to the churches! He who is victorious cannot be harmed
> by the second death," (Revelation 2:7-11, NEB).

"Who was dead and came to life again!" "How hard
pressed you are!" "For ten days you will suffer cruelly!"
It was incredible.

I said, "That's me!" The second attempt at electrocution had killed me, but God had brought me back to
life again. It was *all* right there, the amazing Word of
God which had come to pass in my life. I had died, but
was alive forevermore.

Another verse added excitement to the passage in
Revelation:

> "I have been crucified with Christ, and I myself no longer
> live, but Christ lives in me. And the real life I now have within
> this body is a result of my trusting in the son of God who loved
> me and gave himself for me," (Galatians 2:20, TLB).

The same *forever life* with Jesus was not just for me; it was for everyone who would believe. Out of those words, I began having an insatiable desire to experience all that He had for me and to share that great good news with everyone around me.

I knew I had to learn more before I could be an effective witness, and He began teaching me through so many avenues.

In the weeks and months which followed, God sent me to different people and churches where He nourished my spirit. One of them was the minister at Melle's church. Every evening for a month I went to his church to be taught.

One day I said to him, "Why do you think I had to go through such a holocaust to get to know Jesus and love Him the way I do now?"

Before he could answer me, Jesus whispered the answer in my spirit: "It doesn't matter what you have to go through, because I have you by the hand. It's how you come out of it that counts."

I had just heard the answer from Jesus when the minister said, "Petti, it isn't what you go through that counts — but how you come out of it."

My mouth fell open. When I explained to him what had happened, we shared our amazement. It was the kind of thing we would share many times. The minister and I would often hear God's reply in almost exactly the same words.

"Lord," the minister prayed one day, "why do you let Dr. Wagner, just starting her relationship with You, hear Your voice so clearly so soon? It has taken me twenty years to get where she is already."

"She read the last chapter first," God explained. "I had to give her a crash course."

It was true. God was teaching me so quickly, through our 3 a.m. training sessions, through the people with whom I came in contact, through my nightly visits to church.

I was extreme, I knew. Not everyone could go to such lengths. I had been through so much, I just wanted to know as much as possible, to experience as much as possible with the Lord. It really was a crash course.

There is a joke among many believers — that the young Christian should be locked up for at least six months. I was like that. I couldn't contain my fervency. I *had* to tell everyone about Jesus. The "trouble" with me — I just never got it out of my system. My life seemed like it was just starting on a spiritual roller coaster. Every day the ride gained momentum.

The Father, Son, and Holy Spirit ministered to me daily from three until six o'clock each morning. I was taught spiritual truths, then shown how to minister them to others. Each day I would type out those instructions and see how many of them I could use in my business.

I was led like a child. They explained the basic doctrines about the three baptisms: the born-again experience of being baptized into the Body of Christ by the Holy Spirit; the baptism for repentance by immersion in water; and the baptism in the Holy Spirit, conducted by Jesus Himself as the Baptizer.

They not only explained these things to me so simply that I could not fail to understand them; they also gave me many different Scriptures concerning each baptism, each reinforcing my understanding.

The little Bible Melle had given me was my constant companion. I slept with it on my bed (in fact, since I learned that there was "power in His Word," I put several Bibles around me for protection — again quite extreme, but the basic thought was right). When I left the house, it went with me in my purse. By that time, the bodyguard and his German Shepherd watchdog were all who remained downstairs at night. I was still jumpy and frightened. I knew it would take time to get over that.

I was so excited about everything I was learning about the power of God, that I couldn't help telling others. I wanted them to know. So many Christians didn't know anything about His power.

And every time I would start talking about what He had done for me, things happened. When I told people about the little "lost sheep" prayer the Holy Spirit instructed me to utter to get me back into the fold, they wanted to pray the same prayer. And I figured, if it worked for me, it ought to work for them.

It was the same way with other things. Since God had instructed me to go to church each night for a month, I thought everyone else should do the same when they became Christians.

When I began sharing with others — especially with my clients at Maritronics — what the Lord had taught me about the three baptisms, many of them came to the Lord. My office became my witnessing room.

When I showed people my new eye and all the work which had been done on my fingers and mouth, they became hungry for miracles.

I was just extreme enough to believe Mark 16.18 — that when I laid hands on the sick, they would see miracles, too. Many experienced remarkable recoveries, just like in the Bible!

During those early days of my new walk with Him, the Lord kept pointing me to Scriptures on many different subjects.

He gave me more than two hundred verses about angels. I learned that angels played a very prominent role in God's plan for my life, awaiting only His command (not mine!) to bring me whatever He wanted me to have.

Psalm 35:5 read, "Let them (my enemies) be as chaff before the wind: and let the angel of the Lord chase them." King David had asked God to send angels to chase away the enemies he couldn't handle. If David, why not me?

One day the teaching was about anointing with oil. Well, I wasn't going to do anything half-way. When a friend brought me a gallon of olive oil from the Garden of Gethsemane, I anointed everything in sight — including my office chair.

When He impressed me to read Hebrews 9:14-19, I began covering everything verbally with the blood of Jesus.

I wanted to put the Word into practice. I mean, if it was there, why shouldn't I be a faithful "doer" of the Word?

And God's most frequent instruction to me was always, "Petti, you take the first step, and I will lead you by the hand every step of the way."

I was realizing more than ever that He had ordered my steps all my life, even though I had failed him many times. The anointing He told me about — it *had* been on my life from the beginning. I could look back many times and see that He had given me courage when others backed away. When I started each new venture, He had given me the wisdom to seek the best financial and legal advice available. And even when they counseled me not to start a business, I had sometimes had a "gut" instinct (I didn't know that He was leading me). Time after time, my "hunches" had proven right.

I thought my successes were because I was willing to work harder than others, or because of my rule of thumb — "If people can get more value than they pay for, if *has* to work."

I was learning that my successes had been because God had been directing me — even when I hardly knew Him.

The crash course continued. I remained pretty extreme, even for a Charismatic Christian. But the lessons I was learning were preparing me for much greater tests.

CHAPTER 20

My Son, My Son

One day God impressed me to turn to Hebrews 4:16. I read, "Let us therefore come boldly unto the throne of grace, that we may obtain mercy, and find grace to help in time of need."

Did I have needs? Indeed I had. Did I need help? Yes!

Only God could make a way where there seemed to be no way in some of my situations.

Even though I was seeing financial miracles every day, I found that I *had* to have them. With legal battles shaping up, and with many of my creditors getting "itchy," it was becoming crucial for God to show me answers.

And one of the worst situations concerned Peter, my son. My thoughts were continually with him. I continued to go out each night to Montrose and Drew Streets to pray for my thin, bearded son.

Kimberli came home almost every weekend, and I could tell from our conversation that she was frantic about Peter, too.

Early one morning in June, the door bell rang.

Peter stood there in the doorway. One look told me he had been through his own hell.

"Mother ... Mother ... Mother," he sobbed, flinging himself into my arms. His captors had left town that day, he said, having finally acknowledged that the plot against me would bear no more fruit, only failure and death.

My tears washed away my own loss. I wept for the agonies he had endured. And I began my sincere thanksgiving that God had brought Peter safely home at last.

Then came the real shocker — when we drove to pick up his belongings in the deserted apartment where he had been held, Peter directed me to the intersection of Montrose and Drew Streets, the precise corner where the Holy Spirit had been sending me every night! For six weeks I had gone there to intercede for my son.

"The only time my mind was clear and not affected by the drugs was when I would look through the window and see you parked outside," he told me. "I didn't dare say a word, because for all I knew, they would have grabbed you and killed us both."

Peter, my son. For whatever reason he had initially gotten involved in the plot, he had become a mere pawn in the treacherous scheme.

But why had Peter been released that day instead of being killed by his captors? In my heart, I believed that he was safe because God was faithful to His Word. The Scripture He had given me, insuring my safety — the salvation of all my household, had come to pass. How could I help but praise Him more?

With Peter out of danger, with our family together and mending, my former courage and zest for life returned in giant waves.

But in spite of my faith and fervent prayers, the healing of my jangled nerves was proving to be a slow process. Noises which had gone completely unnoticed for years would suddenly wake me up in stark terror. When the gulf wind was blowing, the TV antenna on the roof sent eerie noises down the wall into my bedroom. That was enough to scare me out of my skin.

It was understandable, I suppose, for someone who had gone through such trauma to have jagged nerves. Still, I felt like God could heal everything.

Then I discovered that God had a perfect remedy, even for nerves.

CHAPTER 21

A New Woman

All during the month of June, the Lord kept urging me to spend the Fourth of July in Acapulco, so that He could heal my nerves. For a while I listened to Him with only half an ear, knowing I couldn't afford such a trip. But each day I was reminded that a trip to Acapulco was part of His plan for my recuperation. When I could no longer ignore those reminders, I began making excuses.

"But Father," I protested, "I don't have anything to wear for such a trip."

Money was coming in better, but I felt obliged to apply all of it to the monstrous credit card debt. My wardrobe was nearly "zilch," especially since my closet had been cleaned out during those terror-filled days.

He finally told me to turn to Matthew 6:28-32—

> "And why be anxious about clothes? Consider how the
> lilies grow in the fields; they do not work, they do not spin; and
> yet, I tell you, even Solomon in all his splendour was not
> attired like one of these. But if that is how God clothes the

grass in the fields, which is here today, and tomorrow is thrown on the stove, will he not all the more clothe you? How little faith you have! No, do not ask anxiously, 'What are we to eat? What are we to drink? What shall we wear?' All these are things for the heathen to run after, not for you, because your heavenly Father knows that you need them all," (NEB).

I was ashamed to mention my limited wardrobe again. And though I still believed that I couldn't afford to make the trip, every day the Lord told me that, in addition to healing for my nerves, I was also going to Acapulco to meet the man of my life — in person!

I wondered what he would be like and I could hardly wait to meet him. That had been my one request during the final moments of my escape.

One day the mailman brought me a letter from the American Express Company. They thanked me for assuming responsibility for the fraudulent charges made to my account. Enclosed with the letter was an American Express Gold Card which put a large line of credit to my disposal.

Not that it really changed anything, or so I thought. It was taking everything I had to keep up with payments on the staggering debts.

Somehow the card seemed connected to my trip to Acapulco. But charge something like that without the funds? That hardly made good business sense. I would never recommend such a step to someone else.

"Lord," I said, "this is so beautiful — to receive the card from American Express — but who is going to pay the bill?"

"I will pay," He affirmed.

It seemed so strange, but I felt a continued leading to make plans for the flight. I was still bothered about my lack of a suitable wardrobe. The black pantsuit I was wearing when kidnapped had become almost a uniform. The only other outfit was a beige and brown tailored pantsuit which my daughter had outgrown.

When friends used to ask me what to take to wear in Acapulco, I would tell them, "All you need is a swimsuit, a smile, and a large dose of sunshine!" Well, with my financial condition, I was traveling almost that lightly.

The Lord detailed instructions for my trip, even down to the hotel where I made reservations.

So it seemed slightly unusual, when I arrived in Acapulco, that God directed me to leave my baggage with the bellman at my hotel and go at once to Las Brisas Hotel.

"Hmmm?" I couldn't imagine the Lord wanting me to meet the man of my life in one of the Las Brisas restaurants or nightclubs. When I arrived at the Las Brisas, a beautiful resort facility built at the foot of the mountain, the Holy Spirit directed my attention up the mountain to the large lighted cross shining out over the city.

"Go to the top," the Lord said. My heart was beating wildly with excitement. I felt sure that in a few moments I would meet the man of my life!

I gave my instructions to the cabdriver and he began the ascent, past the honeymoon cottages nestled into the slopes, up the winding road which led to the lofty ridge where a little chapel provided the anchor for the cross which served as a beacon to the city.

Halfway to the top we came to a guard stationed at a gate across the road. Stopping the cab, the driver informed me that we could go no farther — but I knew better. My Father had taught me well that He will never direct any of His children to do anything or to go anywhere without providing the way.

Jumping out of the cab, I addressed the guard in a tone of authority: "Let us through," I said. "God wants me to go to the top of the mountain." The strange look on his face told me the Lord must have been giving him the very same message. At any rate, the man put up no argument. He simply unlocked the gate and beckoned us through.

As we reached the top, the cross on the lovely little chapel seemed to be twinkling out a welcoming signal especially for me. Bubbling with excitement, I stepped out of the cab and headed for the chapel door. I wondered if the man of my life would be on his knees. Perhaps he would be praying to meet his spouse, too.

With a heart-stopping expectancy, I opened the small door to the chapel. Quickly, my eyes scanned the pews. There was no one. The place was empty. I was crestfallen.

I took another step into the building, and my eyes were enraptured by a full-sized statue of Jesus. I certainly don't believe in worshipping statues, but for an instant He seemed to be alive, illumined with the rosy glow of God's glory all around Him.

Then, in a clear voice which reverberated through the chapel — unmistakably the voice of my Heavenly Father — came the words: "This is the Man of your life."

Something unexplainable happened to me. The presence of God swept through the little building with an awesome power. I fell to the floor. Lying prostrate with my face against the cool tile, I cried and cried and cried. Rivers of tears wet the floor. With every tear, God washed away more of me, making more room for Him.

Every bit of rancor I had ever felt, every condemnation ever placed on me, and all the hurts of the past months which I thought could never be healed, were forever and completely lifted away as I lay there sobbing.

When I felt released to get up, I stood in awe. Checking my watch, I saw that two hours had passed. The time seemed like seconds.

Somehow I knew that all the miracles God had done *for* me in the past were inconsequential compared to the work He had just done *in* me. I knew then that all the overhauling He had accomplished during the previous three months had just been a preliminary to the total cleansing and purifying.

I was healed inside and out. I knew that nothing in the world would ever really matter again — nothing compared to the fact that I belonged to the Man of my life — Jesus.

As a psychologist who had worked with thousands of hurting people, I knew that one of the greatest needs in the human heart was merely to belong.

I *belonged* to Him. I knew it beyond the proverbial shadow of a doubt.

When I finally emerged from the chapel, the cab was still waiting there for me. Still somewhat in a daze, I directed the driver to take me back to my hotel. When we arrived there, I started to pay him. He absolutely refused to take anything!

"I should pay you for the privilege," he said. "I feel like I have been in the presence of Jesus up there."

"So I wasn't the only person who felt Him," I thought. That was just another confirmation to me.

"I *knew* I had!"

I expected the rest of my holiday to be anticlimactic but my Father outdid Himself with each passing day.

I was able to use a white jeep (I took off the top, like my convertible back home, so I called it my "Acapulco Cadillac"), and I drove it from one end of the island to the other. God's glorious sunshine enveloped me, healing every nerve. I praised Him, worshipped Him, sang with Him. For the first time since my kidnapping, I realized that I was able to enjoy nights of peaceful, uninterrupted sleep.

Daily the Holy Spirit led me through every nook and cranny of the area, often directing me to the lovely church in the square. Whenever I headed the jeep that way I knew there would be something special going on.

One morning at church I found myself seated beside

a beautiful native woman. Her daughter was getting married that evening so she invited me to the ceremonies on the spacious tropical lawn beside the ocean. It was such a personal touch — like being in a Mexican paradise.

On another morning, I was sitting under a grass cabana ordering my breakfast. Three handsome gentlemen were at a nearby table. One of them came over — "We can't help noticing your happy face. Won't you please join us for breakfast? We need a touch of your sunshine."

I found that they were the captain, medical officer, and purser of an Australian ship docked in the Acapulco harbor. The ship, on its way around the world, was to stay in the port three more days.

We laughed through breakfast; then they invited me to have dinner on the ship that evening. I accepted and as the orange-tinged sunset emblazoned the Mexican sky, a car was sent for me; then, a ship-to-shore boat took me to the docked vessel.

The evening was as delightful as breakfast had been. As it turned out, we spent much time together during the next days. They were fascinated with the miracles God had performed for me, and God used those miracles to open their hearts to His love. Before I left the ship all three men had invited Jesus to come in and rule their lives!

One of the pieces of jewelry that had been stolen from me was a lovely gold medallion of Jesus' face that a friend had brought me from the Holy Land years before. I had worn it on a gold bar around my neck for so long that I still automatically reached for it every morning. Then would come the abrupt realization that it was gone. Each time my Father would tell me that when I earned it He would provide me with another one, much nicer than the first.

In Acapulco the Holy Spirit took me to all the best

jewelry stores until I found the largest and most beautiful medallion of Jesus' face I had ever seen. It was
pure gold and I felt I couldn't afford it. But then the
Holy Spirit reminded me that God had promised to pay
my American Express account. He seemed to be suggesting that He now judged me ready to receive a
replacement for the medallion that had been stolen. I
wondered what I had done to deserve it.

"Don't you know," He said, "that Jesus is smiling
about the three new souls you introduced to Him —
the captain, the ship's doctor, and the purser?" Afterward, every morning as I hung the medallion around
my neck, I remembered that Jesus smiles whenever I
introduce a new soul to my Heavenly Father.

When it came time for me to leave the resort I was
awakened by the Holy Spirit and told to reconfirm my
reservations for the return trip to the States.

"God, that's old-fashioned. I don't have to do that
anymore. My ticket is all paid for and there's no need
to reconfirm."

Well, I loaded my baggage into my "Acapulco Cadillac" and drove to the airport. When I arrived and checked
my things I was informed that all the seats were
taken.

"But I have a confirmed reservation," I insisted.

"We are sorry," the uniformed agent replied warily.
"A new policy just went into effect. It's necessary to
reconfirm all flights — even passengers with prepaid
tickets."

My heart sank. The Holy Spirit had been right — as
always. If only I had listened to Him!

I was directed out to the airport lawn where I joined a
milling crowd of others who had failed to reconfirm.
The plane on which we planned to leave was nearby,
but the gate was already closed.

"Another plane will be arriving from the States in
several hours," we were told. "Many of you may be able

to return on it."

I was standing in the middle of the restless throng. The pilot suddenly emerged from the plane, walked through the crowd, and came directly to me. Without a word, he took me by the hand and led me up the ramp onto the plane. Inside, he directed me to the only empty seat.

Shocked! I was overcome. Why was I, out of all those people, chosen for this particular flight? It just didn't seem to make sense.

The answer came just minutes before takeoff. God brought to my mind something else which had happened on the island. One day in church I had seen an old beggar woman. Something prompted me to give her my last cash, two dollars. No sooner had I given the money than the Holy Spirit let me know that I had just made a donation to the richest woman in all Acapulco. That made me laugh — "Well, that's all right. She may be the richest beggar in all Acapulco but she loves You very much. Just look at the large bouquet of roses she has placed on Your altar."

On the plane God let me see that because of my pure heart in that act of giving He wouldn't leave me stranded.

How carefully God had planned it all. He let me be relaxed, even though I went on a trip with almost no cash in my purse. He took away my anxiety about the expense. The people I touched and to whom I witnessed — they were part of the plan, too.

The nervousness about noises in the night? In the light of His perfect love for me, that was gone forever. The Man in my life made it as if it had never been.

All in all it was a new woman who came back to Houston to resume God's work.

God was getting me ready for the great tasks still ahead.

CHAPTER 22

Preparations

There is a path each new "baby" Christian takes on the road to maturity. Too often we tend to judge new believers for their own sometimes-bizarre steps.

I went through so many different stages. There was the radio evangelist who offered to evaluate a person's spiritual condition for a twenty-five dollar fee (I made an appointment with him, but the Lord let me know that it was a spiritual detour, that the man was actually involved in the occult).

I attended a church where the pastor had "prove me" offerings. I gave a lot of money there as I tried to seek God's guidance. Finally I was shown the error of paying for God's direction.

I took instruction in one of the liturgical churches, though I was shown some of that institution's errors. Still, I was a baby Christian and I was eager to grow up into the fullness of all God had planned for me.

Just like a teenager who tries to put his arms around the whole world at one time, I was trying to learn everything about God at once.

Still, the power of God, which had been visible as light around me that day of my escape, continued to be manifest in unusual ways.

During the year following my kidnapping, many people who had cancer sat in my office. Sometimes the Holy Spirit would heal them even before I could lay hands on them!

God began moving me in other directions. The healing ministry wasn't withdrawn but the healings began to come less often as sudden, spontaneous manifestations, and more frequently in a gradual process as persons learned to exercise their faith in God's Word.

Meanwhile, I continued my roller-coaster ride. During the transition period I experienced notable highs and lows in many things — my finances, my zest for life, my determination to serve the Lord.

One evening, while I was having a "pity party," I felt an urge for something liquid to ease the pressures. I drove to a hotel near my office and ordered an exotic mixed drink. Many times in the past, after an especially grueling day, I had stopped there for a cocktail to pick up my falling emotions, but that was the first time since my kidnapping that I felt the need for anything like that. While I waited for my drink to arrive I kept my thoughts running as low as possible, continuing to feel sorry for myself and the shape I was in.

"Well, Lord," I sighed, "I suppose You'll be taking away my cocktails, too. Everything else seems to be gone."

But after only one sip I *had* to put it down. It tasted like bitter vetch! I had never been a heavy drinker but I knew I would never take a drink again.

In my despondency I told God that I felt my life was just about over and suggested that He give what remained of it to a child for whom I had been praying, a seven-year-old boy with leukemia.

God's answer to my offer snapped me out of my dejection: "It's not your life to give," He said firmly and kindly. "You cannot run away from life, you cannot run away from death, you cannot run away from God, you cannot run away from yourself. I have these four walls built around you so high that you cannot climb over them. Now get up and fight."

The words were like an irresistable challenge. There was so much to be done. There were so many who wanted to give up on life. I began feeling such a strong desire to help them to live.

Above all things I wanted to be pleasing to Him, even during the low moments.

As I grew, God directed me to a special fellowship (Lakewood Church) and a compassionate pastor (John Osteen). The messages I heard there were so simple, so profound. They reached down and touched people where they lived. I needed that. I needed the right kind of teaching to help me between the peaks and valleys.

During those years I took theology classes at Rice University, I attended numerous fellowships and Bible studies, I watched Christian programs.

Somehow God was able to use the hodgepodge for His glory.

It was all just a matter of going through those stages toward maturity. Some, I found, are reluctant to grow in the Christian walk. But God holds us responsible, not for what we have, but could have; not for what we are, but might be.

I would need every bit of encouragement, each fiber of strength, and lots of determination to make it through the coming months.

Perhaps the biggest battle of my life lay just ahead.

CHAPTER 23

Vengeance

By the spring of 1974 Jerry Hamilton had everything ready for trial of our major case — our suit against the hospital on Westheimer.

To that point, everything had been decided in our favor. Even the suit against Dr. Ronald Holmes, the man who had authorized that savage "treatment," had been settled out of court. There was no question that he had divested himself from acceptable standards of care, but the legal battles would have outweighed the benefits of a full-blown court battle with the doctor. At that time, malpractice suits were seldom in favor of the patient, no matter how bad the treatment had been. Juries still seemed to look at doctors as infallible. So, when Dr. Holmes' lawyer and Jerry agreed to very liberal terms, the suit was dropped. To me, it was more than the money Holmes had to pay; the settlement was a moral victory, too.

Plus, the biggest struggle was the suit against the hospital where I had been tortured and murdered.

The preparation for the court date reached a fever pitch. In fact, because of my research skills, I was able to help Jerry track down similar cases. I came back with reams of material for the battle.

When the date was set, I said, "Lord, I didn't know I'd have to go to court to get my own money back."

His reply was, "Are you on trial?"

I thought a minute and said, "No, Lord."

"Do not be afraid. I will send my angels before you," He said.

Thus, when the actual trial began, God sent different people to stay in the courtroom and pray: a bishop from Galveston, a group of believers from Tulsa, an archbishop from Canada, and some of the well-known television ministers.

The three-week trial, "Olive Peet Wagner vs. Southwest General Hospital," was a travesty in some ways, a series of shocks in other ways.

The judge had a real problem with me. I couldn't help being edgy and indignant each time different people were brought to the stand, especially when they told deliberate lies. The judge wanted me to sit quietly, not even to talk to my attorney. I was wrong with my initial outbursts, but I hardly deserved the eagle-eye treatment he gave me.

For three horrible weeks, it dragged on and on. Each night I slumped home. It looked like an impossible task — to take on a major hospital and prove negligence. Only by reading God's Word could I gain enough strength to face the next day. Family members gave me hope. Jerry Hamilton remained optimistic, but I wondered if he were keeping his spirits high just for my benefit.

Jerry had done his homework. He was an eloquent courtroom lawyer. His treatment of the depositions and materials kept the jury and audience alert.

There were lighter moments. The Follower, one of

my guards, gave the story of my escape: "Judge, it had to have been an inside job. No woman in Dr. Wagner's condition could have taken down the wall. It took six men to put it back up!" The whole courtroom broke into laughter at the way he said it.

When the Follower said that, I leaned over to Jerry and whispered, "It *was* an inside job, all right. God, Jesus, and the Holy Spirit helped me remove that wall. But if I say *that*, they'll have me locked up again quicker than anything!"

There were the eerie moments. We had to subpoena things from the hospital, including the wig stand. When Dr. Holmes produced that, with the words inscribed, I almost felt dizzy from the emotions it produced.

Skinny testified. She didn't help the defense much when she gustily described how she jabbed the injections — "We did it right through her black blouse!"

Steel-and-Thunder was there, too. As it turned out, once Jerry started cross-examining him, the blubbery giant proved to be one of our best witnesses. Jerry asked him about the electroshock, and the slow-talking hulk proudly described how a person, like me, often flopped around and fell off the "meat wagon" and onto the floor when the "juice" was turned on.

My physician, Dr. John McGuire, gave a deposition which proved to be useful:

Q—Did you specifically contact the hospital?

A—Yes, I did.

Q—And what happened when you talked to them?

A—Well, they refused to give me any information at all concerning her, and I demanded that I talk with the supervisor of nursing. I don't recall what her name was, but she identified herself as the supervisor of nursing in charge at that time. I explained to her who I was, that I was this person's personal physician, and would like to speak to her, and she refused to even give me the

room number or permission to see the patient whatsoever.

Q—Were you able to find out from her who her physician was? Who was treating her?

A—No. I never did find that out either.

Q—Did you make some attempts then to contact
any of her friends and relatives or something?

A—Yes, I did. As a matter of fact, I stayed up most of
the night making calls to different people ...

Q—From the observations that you have had of Mrs.
Wagner, both socially and in your office, has it been of
such a nature that if she had a severe psychiatric
disorder, it would be apparent to you?

A—That's right.

Q—All right, sir. When you saw her on March the 6th,
was her behavior on that occasion consistent with
what you had observed of her before?

A—Exactly the same. My employees didn't notice
anything unusual about her either.

Q—Specifically, did she, in your opinion, require
hospitalization and psychiatric treatment on the 6th of
March, the last time you saw her?

A—Definitely not.

Q—On the 6th of March did she require, in your
opinion, hospitalization for anything?

A—No sir.

The basic assumption behind all the treatment was
that I did need psychiatric care, that Peter signed for
me to be detained for such care, and that I had even
given Dr. Holmes a written consent for what transpired.

Dr. Holmes' deposition told quite another story:

Q—Did you obtain her consent to have Convulsive
Therapy or any electrical current administered to
her?

A—No, I know now we did not.

Q—Did she sign any written consent? Did you ever

ask her to sign a written consent according to the law?

A—No, I realize now that I never did receive her permission.

Q—When you asked for her son to sign such a slip did you know that it was 3 days after she had been electrocuted, had come back to life, and had escaped from her prison.

A—Yes, I know it now.

Q—Did you know that her son was under the influence of drugs at this time.

A—Yes, I know it now.

Q—Yet you asked him to sign this permit three days after this had been done. The paper that she should have signed before electricity could ever be applied to her.

A—Yes, I did.

Q—Do you have a copy of it with you?

A—Yes, I do.

Q—What is the date on that?

A—The date is 3-22-71.

Q—In spite of all these reports on your records reflecting her presence on the 18, 19, 20, 21, and 22, you do realize that she escaped at three a.m. on the 18th of March 1971?

A—Yes, I know it now.

Q—Who could have falsified these records with your signature?

A—I suppose the nurse on duty.

Q—What kind of current was the voltage you used?

A—I can tell you that the voltage is — you want it specifically in this treatment?

Q—This treatment.

A—This treatment. I think it was an old machine from the store room and it was without the controls. It is 240 volts. Ordinarily the machine is from 150 to 170. I don't know how this old worn out machine happened to be used.

Q—Do you know the amperage?

A—No I do not. It is supposedly a low amperage but this machine had no gauges or controls.

Q—In this particular case, did her body jump? Was there a ...

A—Yes, her body lunged and convulsed and then her heart stopped.

Q—Did she ever indicate to you during the time that she was there that she wanted to see Dr. John McGuire, her personal physician?

A—I don't recall.

Q—Do you recall during the time she was there that you ordered her a black wig?

A—Yes.

Q—What color was her hair when she arrived at the hospital?

A—It was black.

Q—Do you recall the color of her hair when she was declared dead?

A—It was snow white.

Q—Wasn't it slightly unusual for electricity to change the color of anyone's hair.

A—Yes.

The jury heard the evidence. Each attorney gave his closing arguments. The judge gave his final instructions. When the jury reappeared, we waited breathlessly for the result. The *Final Judgment* relates the overwhelming victory. Jury members agreed that there had been a premeditated kidnapping, that I had been held without legal consent, that I had been injected with drugs against my will, that I had been given electroshock treatments without legal authorization, and that I had suffered severe bodily injury. The jury ruled in favor of me on every count!

The *Final Judgment* was rendered on March 6, 1974, just two days shy of the third anniversary of my

NO. ~~████████~~

MRS. OLIVE P. WAGNER	X	IN THE DISTRICT COURT OF
	X	
V.	X	HARRIS COUNTY, T E X A S
	X	
~~████~~ GENERAL HOSPITAL,	X	
INC., ET AL	X	JUDICIAL DISTRICT

SATISFACTION AND RELEASE OF JUDGMENT

THAT WHEREAS, on the 25th day of March, 1974, in the above
and foregoing cause, Mrs. Olive P. Wagner recovered a judgment
against   General Hospital, a Texas corporation, in the
sum of ~~─────────────────~~ with interest thereon
at the rate of six per cent (6%) per annum from March 25, 1974,
together with all costs of Court; and

WHEREAS, the said judgment has been fully and finally paid
to the undersigned, Mrs. Olive P. Wagner, and at the time of its
payment, the said undersigned was the legal and equitable owner
and holder of said judgment, and the party fully entitled to
receive payment thereof;

NOW, THEREFORE, KNOW ALL MEN BY THESE PRESENTS, that Mrs.
Olive P. Wagner, in consideration of the payment of said judgment
together with interst and court costs, hereby acknowledges and
admits full and complete payment of the above-described judgment,
and does hereby release unto the said ~~████~~ General Hospital,
and Argonaut Southwest Insurance Company, their successors
and assigns, such judgment and any and all liens, claims and de-
mands heretofore existing by reason thereof upon any of the property of the said   General Hospital and Argonaut Southwest
Insurance Company, whatsoever.

WITNESS MY HAND this 24 day of ____Tens____, 1974.

[signature]
Mrs. Olive P. Wagner

APPROVED AND PAYMENT ACKNOWLEDGED:

[signature]
Attorney for Plaintiff,
Mrs. Olive P. Wagner

kidnapping.

The *Satisfaction and Release of Judgment* was handed down on March 25, 1974. Ironically, the Insurance Company for the hospital said, "We insured you against malpractice. We did not insure you against kidnapping. We will not pay." That left the hospital to pay the bill. Unfortunately, the hospital owner's brothers were 1) a prominent judge and 2) a prominent lawyer. When Jerry went to the Judge's Chambers on March 25, he had to wait because the judge was in conference. He found out the reason for the delay — out of the Judge's Chambers walked the two brothers (the lawyer and the judge). They had been in conference with the judge assigned to my trial.

Thus, behind a closed-door session without Jerry Hamilton present, the payment was substantially reduced. It was an obvious agreement between friends — the judge and the two brothers. It had happened before. Is there something wrong with our jurisprudence?

But, at least we had won! I had been called crazy, mentally incompetent, and senile. The problem with such accusations, even when flippantly made by psychiatrists or drug-influenced people, are that they are next to impossible to disprove — "Guilty until proven innocent!"

I had never gone through anything like that before. The mental trauma from the accusations was enough to break a person. Those slanders, on top of the physical damage, had almost destroyed me.

So it was as much a personal victory for me as it was an indictment on the hospital and on the state licensing system that would allow such an atrocity to happen.

God had promised victory. Why had I ever doubted Him?

I wanted to savor the taste of victory, but there was

much to be done.

CHAPTER 24

Living Witness

The story hardly ended with the "impossible" victory in court.

There were numerous other lawsuits as well — against the medical staff of the hospital on Westheimer, against the persons who stole all my property, against the psychiatrists at the county hospital (who were involved in a money-in-the-pocket scam), and against others involved in the cold-blooded scheme. In each case, the victory was ours.

God's Word was confirmed — I had victory against every lie, and no weapon formed against me would prosper (Isaiah 54:17).

Meanwhile, God's judgment against the conspirators mounted. In addition to the four who died as I made my escape — David, Theodore (in the same plane as David), George, and Don — there were others. Zelda, whom I never saw again, was tracked from California to Denver to New York; she died of an overdose of heroin before she had much of a chance to enjoy all her "profits." Steel-and-Thunder died of a stroke not long after he testified in court. The judge who reduced the amount of damages the jury had awarded me died the next week after his actions. The attorney who collected some of my insurance dishonestly was disbarred and can no longer practice law in the state of Texas. The judge who illegally gave Peter power of attorney had a severe heart attack and had to be fitted with a pacemaker.

Strange? A mere series of coincidences? I hardly think so. I don't believe in coincidences where God's children are concerned. His Word is so plain on the subject, that He will bless those who bless His people (Genesis 12:30), and bring woe to those who touch the apple of His eye (Zechariah 2:8-9).

The saddest part is that my kidnappers, by their involvement in a plot against a Christian, had aligned themselves with evil, setting themselves up to share in Satan's destruction. They had chosen death when a loving God had offered them life.

My only hope is that those involved who are still living will find the truth before it is too late for them.

Further, I wish I could say that the court victory marked the end of all my problems. Humans are like that — we want all the success stories to end with someone walking off in fleecy clouds of bliss.

Hardly. I was robbed twice by a fellow who went to our church in Houston. Quite frankly, after the second time, I got mad. I began praying, "Lord, whoever that person is, I ask You to make him confess." I earnestly travailed for the person for an entire week. He had robbed 15 people in our church. It just seemed so wrong. And sure enough, before the week ended, he called the police from a Corpus Christi Dairy Queen and told them everything!

Not long after the trial, God told me to go to Methodist Hospital to pray for Reverend John Osteen, who

was scheduled for open-heart surgery. Grateful for
the ministry this man had in Houston, I felt honored to
be asked. By this time, I had seen God perform many
miracles for people when I prayed for them, and I
wanted to be an instrument of His healing love any
time I could. My morning prayer was always, "Lord,
clean my channel completely free of any thought or
deed or hindrance that is not of You, and forgive me for
all my unrighteousness. Make my channel so pure
that You can pour the fullness of Your Love through
me and use it for Your glory. Lord, use me any way You
wish."

I was eager to go and pray for Pastor Osteen, but all
the way to the hospital I fretted about the parking
situation. "Lord, You know I cannot park there," I com-
plained, thinking of the narrow ramp leading to the
hospital and the only slightly wider road at the foot of it
— neither of them designed for parking.

But God sent me to the hospital when the traffic was
lightest, and I pulled right into the empty space directly in front of the main entrance — in a zone marked
"ABSOLUTELY NO PARKING. TOWING ENFORCED."
Just as I feared, a policeman approached me as soon
as I had come to a stop. But instead of insisting that I
move on, he seemed to be reading the bumper stick-
ers on the front and back of my Cadillac, proclaiming
"PRAISE JESUS" and "JESUS LOVES YOU." Then he
greeted me with a smile instead of the stern warning
for which I had prepared myself.

"May I stop here a few minutes to pray for a precious
man of God who's scheduled for open-heart surgery?"
I asked him.

"Not only that," he said, his dark eyes twinkling back
at me, "I'll even watch over your car for you if you want
to go inside and lay hands on him."

Four times a day for three days — early in the morning before I went to the office, at noon, in the evening

at dinner time, and again at eleven o'clock at night when I had finished the day's work — I drove to the same spot, parked my car, and sat there interceding for Brother Osteen.

I was certain that he had many other people praying for him, but I knew I had been called as a special intercessor to maintain a hotline to God for him while he was getting deeper and deeper into his own positive confession that He was healed by God's Word.

On the fourth day, when I drove into the "NO PARK-ING" place God had reserved for me, my policeman walked over to my car. "The man you have been praying for has gone home," he said. "He did not have to have surgery after all." I had never mentioned John Osteen's name to him, so I knew this message must have come from God.

In my excitement at hearing the good news, I reached out my open window, grabbed the officer's neck, and gave him a big hug. All the way back to my office, I praised God and thanked Him for His great mercy in restoring — for my benefit and the benefit of thousands of others — one of the world's great teachers of God's Word.

It was the farthest thing from my mind, but I would soon be needing that kind of mercy for myself.

On November 1, 1975, I went to a women's clinic for my routine annual checkup, but the consequences of that visit were anything but routine. The pap smear showed a positive indication of a malignant cancer of the uterus. I was called in for more tests. The results were the same each time.

But God had other ideas. Three times He had people confirm — with identical words — that I would be healed by the Word of God. The third time was most unusual. God had already prepared a special man who was to pray for me. Is it any wonder that He led me to go to intercede for Reverend Osteen when he was ill? John

Osteen didn't know me personally, so I was naturally shocked when, as I sat in the middle of 2000 people at a Thanksgiving service, Reverend Osteen asked, "Is there a Dr. Wagner here?" I replied "Yes!" He then confirmed, "You are healed by the Word of God!"

Just like that! Not only did I have a clean bill of health when I returned to my gynecologist, but also the doctor eventually received Jesus Christ as a result of that healing!

My mouth was another problem. For six years after the beatings I went several times a week to see the man whom God had chosen to do the work. My jaw-bone was made whole by being fused with pulverized sections from one of my ribs. Dr. Frazier built a solid gold roof for my mouth and re-implanted my teeth. He succeeded in saving every original tooth except two.

All the dental students who observed the work in progress were naturally curious to know what had caused those gruesome injuries. As they heard my story, many received the Lord. During those six years, that dental school turned out many, many born-again Christians.

With all of the other miracles, God has not had it in my blueprint to change my single status of 22 years. I divorced to preserve my life and for the psychological well-being of my children. Had I known then what I know today, I could have preserved my own marriage. Had either of us been schooled in the knowledge of God, we would have recognized the work of the devil, whose greatest joy is to send dividing spirits to attack homes. My husband would have taken his rightful place as spiritual head of the family and would have been able to share in the formative years of our children's lives.

It is said that people die from lack of knowledge. It is in the light of this knowledge today, however, that I daily pray for my former husband's salvation. In God's eyes Karl is still part of my household, and I can claim him for the Kingdom of God.

I am certain that the prayers of a righteous woman availeth much; yet, at that time I was not a righteous woman and not equipped with the holy boldness I have today. Now, I am a prayer warrior and a great problem to the devil. Had I had those virtues then, I have no doubt Karl would be born again by now. As a result of the daily "standing in" for his salvation, I am purged of all bitterness and unforgiveness. I am convinced that one day he will be born again.

Nevertheless, with the problems have come an incredible amount of wonderful times.

Both of my children have finished school. Somehow, just as their admission papers were completed each year, the funds would arrive. For the first few years when it happened, Peter and Kimberli thought this provision was only a coincidence, that the money just "happened" to be there when needed. The college money, however, became a revealing witness to them.

Today, Peter is married to his beautiful wife and has a successful real estate business. We share a special love and respect because of everything that happened. That love and respect sometimes seems a bit overwhelming. One day someone said to him, "Your mother is a great woman — but a little flamboyant." Peter came forth as my champion immediately, saying, "No, my mother is *not* flamboyant. She has flair and class."

Yes, I think I like that. I have class in Jesus.

Kimberli is a talented writer, singer, and actress. She is the one who, in my darkest moments, has written notes and poems which were as a gentle balm, such as the following:

To Mom,

All my love.

I love you mostly because you are thoughtful in your thoughtlessness, patient in your exasperation,

Younger than I can believe I ever was, and wiser than I think I ever could be.

I know that it is when you have no time for me that I am foremost in your thoughts, so that

I know I must be patient with you like you must be patient with me.

I love you because you are sentimental, and to real friends, you are the best of friends.

I love you because you believe in me — whatever I try to do — and when I need you I know you'll be there.

Willing to let me need you and give yourself to me.

I love you because you are exasperatingly unreasonable, *lovable,* a little domineering, *lovable,* kindly, *lovable,* gentle, tactless, *lovable,* dynamic and *lovable.*

But most of all I love you because you are my mother
And a very big part of me.

Your daughter, Kim.

My life has continued to change. I have seen God turn my calamities to good in so many ways. He has used even the scraps of paper I hid under my mattress during the imprisonment. They became resource material for a project at Stanford University, providing insight into the "death syndrome" experienced by many people approaching the end of life.

I am continually learning that God does not object to His children having fine possessions. Since my great loss, He has returned much of what was taken. But the process has just begun. I was promised a restoration in every area of my life.

I live well. Sometimes people cannot understand that. In fact, I have been criticized for wearing so many rings. What people don't know is that God has given me rings to cover the ugly scars from that first horrible night in Room 120.

He provided the exact amount of money for a new Cadillac, right down to the penny, at the last minute, from a forgotten source — insurance money — that was long past due.

When I was led to sell my business and building in Houston, God worked an incredible miracle of last-minute financing for the new owners.

But those are some of the material miracles. I would rather relate the deeper, more lasting things.

God has continued His restoration process in my spirit. It hasn't been a snap. I've worn out many Bibles in my never-ending study to know Him better. I still feel like a brand-new Christian, still on His crash course.

The results of the string of miracles God began long ago in my life are still spreading. I've been fortunate to appear on national television programs and in numerous services and churches.

It's on the one-to-one level, however, that God seems to bless exceedingly.

God has used me many times to reach people close to me. My own attorney, Jerry Hamilton, came back to the Lord as we worked together. I even got to introduce him to his future wife. They now are happily married and have two beautiful children.

Because of my own experiences in the forced imprisonment, it seems I am the one many people call when they hear of similar terror-filled circumstances among loved ones or friends. There is no way of knowing how many totally sane people are unjustly incarcerated in mental institutions and hospitals.

Thankfully, God seems to have a growing network of concerned psychiatrists and experts in the field who are seeing positive changes.

I get a special thrill when God leads me to pray for physical needs, and a bigger thrill when I get letters like the following:

On July 11, I had Melanoma Cancer.
I asked you to pray for me. The Lord gave you a word of knowledge that God's time to manifest my healing was right then. You prayed for me.

> Today is October 13. I have just completed my test at the cancer clinic and the doctor told me he saw nothing on all of the tests. There is no more evidence of cancer. I have a complete healing!!
> (from Shirley, a Louisiana woman)

Or, this note from Evangelist Jimmy Clanton, once a top Rock and Roll recording artist, now a minister of God's Word.

> About two years ago, Dr. Wagner invited my family and me to her home just prior to our departure from Houston. We had become friends through our church.
> She noticed my oldest daughter had a misshaped leg due to a car accident some years before.
> As she talked to Dusty, my daughter agreed to sit and allow Dr. Wagner to pray for her.
> One leg had been shorter than the other, but as Dr. Wagner prayed, Dusty felt a "tugging." When we looked, the leg was perfect! Praise God!

As much as I enjoy being used in healing and helping, my greatest joy is when I lead people to the Lord.

I realize now that God has used all the horrible things in my life to bring me where I am today. In the midst of adversity and suffering, He has kept manifesting His power so that others could come to believe in Him and have everlasting life.

Is it worth it?

Even if only one lost soul had come to a saving knowledge of Jesus, it would have been worth it all.

I don't know why God chose me for my own particular path. I don't think any person can understand why He allows one person to be an heiress while growing up, and another person to be a pauper. Nor can I fathom why people are given special talents in one field or another.

All I know is that I am only responsible for the steps I take — one at a time.

I have found my niche — in Him. Some people seem embarrassed to share His love with others. I just can't understand that anymore. Rev. John Osteen calls me "the greatest soulwinner of our time." Well, I don't know about that. However, I do know how important it is for me to share what I've learned, what has happened to me, what I am.

If that makes me extreme, then so be it. If my daily doses of holy boldness make me "different," then that's the way it has to be.

I don't really have a choice. I've already made that decision. I have many packages left to wrap, many "red ribbons" left to tie.

I sat face-to-face with the Lord Jesus Christ. Then I came back. How can I help but be a living witness?

> O the depth of the riches both of the wisdom and knowledge of God! how unsearchable are his judgments, and his ways past finding out!
>
> For who hath known the mind of the Lord? or who hath been his counsellor?
>
> Or who hath first given to him, and it shall be recompensed unto him again?
>
> For of him, and through him, and to him, are all things: to whom be glory for ever.
> Amen.
>
> I beseech you therefore, brethren, by the mercies of God, that ye present your bodies a living sacrifice, holy, acceptable unto God, which is your reasonable service.
>
> And be not conformed to this world: but be ye transformed by the renewing of your mind, that ye may prove what is that good, and acceptable, and perfect, will of God (Romans 11:33-36, 12:1-2).

For personal correspondence write:

Dr. Petti Wagner
P. O. Box 462
Altamonte, Florida 32715-0462
(305) 339-3553